Book Cover Designed by:
Ojedokun Daniel Olusegun
Dannymedia47@gmail.com

Cover Image by:
Elisheva Liss, LMFT

If you read books like I do, you probably flip to the back to see if there's a photo and bio of the author. Any material is much more interesting to me when I have an idea of where it's coming from. So I'll save you the trouble of flipping to the back and just introduce myself here:

Hi. I'm Elisheva. Or sometimes just Eli, but close relatives call me Sheva. I am an LMFT, which stands for licensed marriage and family therapist, by profession. I am also a wife, mom, daughter, sister, friend, neighbor, writer, teacher, speaker, student, subclinical hoarder, and person who keeps trying to eat healthier  but really likes chocolate and pizza (although generally not together). In my day job, I happen to have an accidental specialty in treating sexual disorders, but that is for another book.

This book you just started to read is sort of a 40th birthday present to myself. A few years ago, I was going through one of my many, many boxes of "old crinkly random stuff," and I came across an essay that I'd written as a little girl. It was one of those "When I grow up" compositions. I had written the following words, decades ago: "When I grow up, I want to be a mommy, a teacher, a therapist, and a writer."

I got the chills when I read that, because apparently, I've had the good fortune to be able to do exactly what I'd wanted as a schoolgirl. I've been blessed with five awesome kids (this is a totally unbiased assessment by their Jewish mother), a decade's worth of teaching high school and college students, a fulfilling psychotherapy practice, and a number of published articles. But it occurred to me that I had always hoped to "one day" write a book. Hitting this midlife hilltop has a way of putting things in perspective, and in my tradition, we have a saying: "If not now, when?" (the equivalent of "there's no time like the present").

While we live in an era of unprecedented public personal expression, exposure, and living out loud, I happen to hail from a community and family culture that values and promotes modesty and privacy. Intellectually, I respect and support those values. But personally, I'm not really built that way. While many of my friends had stage fright, or a fear of public speaking, I always got my surge of adrenaline on center stage and behind the mic. I've always struggled against my innate loudness and arrogance, alternately trying to smother, deny, or sublimate them. I've tried to utilize and reframe them as assertive and confident, but I generally know when I've crossed that line. (Well, at least afterwards. Especially after someone tells me.) So in my public speaking and writing, I've tried to balance my natural tendency to relate by (over)sharing, with a respect for the privacy of all the people with whom my life intersects personally. (My daughter thinks I'm painting myself in a bad light here. Having children is a great way to start a loyal fan base.)

Besides for all of the above, I am also an Orthodox Jew, which, for one thing, means I own quite a lot of cotton maxi skirts. (And throw pillows, but that's not a religious issue, just a personal compulsion I need to work through.) This book is intended for an audience of all faiths, affiliations, and unfaiths, not specifically a religious audience. I love spiritual exploration for myself, but I don't believe in proselytizing. Yet, I'm grateful to have a rich spiritual heritage of historical, Biblical and Talmudic wisdom from which to learn, draw from, and introspect.

Growing up Jewish in New York often carries with it a paradoxical message that sounds something like this: "We are, um, technically, proud of who we are and what we stand for, but… still, maybe try to lay below the radar, because people like to hate us, and beat us up sometimes, so keep it down if you can, don't make too much noise while you're out there being proud of the tribe." On the one hand, there's an identity doctrine, a scrappy survival instinct, and on the other, a shrinking inward, even a sense of shame: "Don't antagonize anyone, and don't embarrass us." Or: "There are a lot of people out there who hate us anyway. Let's not give them any reason to justify it."

Even as I write this, I find myself wondering if it's wise to share it. I am a Jew, but I don't represent all of my people. I am likewise an American, but many of my landsmen disagree with my opinions. But I think the dual-cultural, yin-yang message we absorb is not unique to one group. I think many of us internalize this on a personal level, too:

"Be proud of who you are, be yourself, be unique… but not too unique; like, don't be weird, and don't do things that will make people want to bully you, or cringe, or anything like that—y'know? Just, like, be an individual within specific, socially acceptable parameters, something you can pull off without looking like a freak, ok?" Sort of a tight- rope between individuation and belonging.

I know that I was always confused about my own weirdness. As a little girl, I vividly remember my best friend laughing at my quirkiness and saying, "You're so weird!" and me replying, "Thank you!" I genuinely thought it was a compliment until about fourth grade. But there is such a fine line between unique and abnormal, and I think I spent at least a decade on the wrong side of that line. I still like to hang out there sometimes, because it's often way more fun there and definitely more authentic. (It's also a great way to embarrass your kids.)

My father taught me that the definition of normal is: someone you don't know very well. I think that the only difference between being an individual and being odd is how it all works out for you. My hope is that this book will help people find and embrace their own wonderful weirdness and work it into an asset, rather than bury it as a liability.

I know I have a tendency to be snarky, and I hope that tone gets edited down to propriety. I also hope the words in this book never cause anyone any pain, shame or sorrow. They are designed only to educate and motivate, never to denigrate. But if they ever inadvertently do, please accept my apology. Anything you find of value in these pages is a result of everything I've learned from others over the course of my lifetime: my parents, grandparents, siblings, husband, children, family-in-law, community, teachers, colleagues, supervisors, supervisees, friends, students, clients, a bazillion books, videos, the amazing miracle of the internet, and the "real" world. But I take personal responsibility for and ownership of any flaws, errors, or omissions in this work. They are a reflection of no one and nothing other than my own imperfection.

Narrative therapy, which I will describe in the next couple of chapters, is the clinical modality that speaks to my heart. A narrative is essentially a story. We are each living at the center of a complex story, and simultaneously play many varied supporting roles in the narratives of others. The techniques I share in this book are tools for editing and narrating our stories in more empowered, effective ways. I know that when I'm reading a book, my eye tends to wander away from the theory and toward the vignettes. I imagine I'm not the only one who does that. For that reason, I will try to flavor my theories and information with a hefty dose of human interest and experience, since that's what makes the theory relevant and interesting anyway.

Table of Contents

Introduction

I have some symbolic nature photos displayed in my office, in direct line of view from where my clients sit, and they are often an important part of the work we do.

The main one is a picture of a seagull soaring over refreshingly frothy, aqua waves. I took it on a beach on my first trip to Miami, several years ago.

Another features a sailboat, centered over a calm sea, taken off the coast of Maui.

A third features whitecap breakers, crashing wildly against jagged rocks in Long Beach, five minutes from my home.

At first glance, these are simply soothing, scenic snapshots, and for some of my clients, they stay that way. But for others, it is a visual aid for an important technique. It serves as a useful metaphor for better, healthier living.

So often, I hear a variation of the following problem: "I want to be calm and content, but I just find my mind flooded with unhappy or anxious thoughts and feelings too much of the time. It gets me down or stressed. It's so much my nature that I don't even know if it's possible for me to be any other way." I hear this from clients and friends, but I used to hear it in my own head, too.

Enter the beach pics. The exercise I am about to describe will be developed comprehensively over the course of this book. But the analogy, simplified, goes something like this:

This is a picture of the horizon. The horizon is a horizontal (see the word in there?) line, where the sky meets land or water. On a two dimensional piece of paper, we can easily see the areas below, above or right on the line of the horizon. In our minds, we can try to conceptualize the horizon as a divider between healthy and unhealthy zones of thought. I call this the **Horizon of Healthy Function.**

Imagine a person below the horizon. He has fallen into the swirling waters and is struggling, almost drowning. That is how someone feels when s/he is deeply depressed or desperately anxious, furiously angry, bitingly critical, or bitterly resentful. Sometimes the tone of our thinking becomes so toxically negative and unhealthy that it robs us of the ability to thrive. I call that *below* the Horizon of Healthy Thinking. There is a spectrum of unpleasant emotions that could be swimming there — discouragement, hopelessness, fear, anxiety, frustration, aggravation, anger, rage, and more—but the common denominator between them is a sense that somehow, all is not "OK." I'm not OK, you're not OK, the world is not OK.

Nothing is OK in those moments. All that is below the horizon.

At other times, we are simply in touch with reality as it is. We are neither bogged down by it, nor uplifted by it. It just "is." In our minds and with our words, we "call it like we see it." This is what I call *on* the Horizon of Healthy Function. At times, this is a perfectly good place to be and works quite well. It can be compared to a boat, gently tracing the surface of the water by bobbing along the waves. It's OK.

Finally, there is the seagull, soaring upward, *above* the Horizon. This is when our thought processes take us to a place of good feeling—productivity, serenity, health, or personal growth. And it doesn't need to be profound.

Let's use a very simple, seemingly inconsequential example. I left a message for a colleague, Jeff, a few hours ago regarding a three- way consult with another colleague, Sue, and am waiting to hear back. Sue asks what's happening with the consult.

I could say, "Well, I left Jeff a message a few hours ago, but he hasn't bothered to call me back yet." Hear the miffed tone of that one? Neglected and resentful.

Alternatively, I could say, "I left him a message this morning." Just the facts, ma'am.

Or, "I left him a voicemail this morning, so I'm hoping he heard it and will call back soon. If not, maybe we'll try him again in a few minutes." Matter-of-fact, hopeful, and proactive.

A simple reply to an innocuous question, with three similar versions. And not particularly important in the scheme of things. Yet as a matter of habit, being someone who regularly thinks and speaks like the first will generate negative energy. The second approach is pragmatic and utilitarian. But the third yields good energy and movement.

While I generally use the following terms somewhat interchangeably, Horizon of Healthy Thinking or HHT, usually refers to cognitive thought positioning, while Horizon of Healthy Function or HHF refers to this thought process applied to thought plus some other action or dialogue.

In the chapters of this book, I hope to share ideas and examples of how we can train our minds to operate *above* the horizon of Healthy Function. The benefits are immediate and obvious. How we think becomes what we feel, believe and actualize. Generating a hopeful, empowered, productive way of relating to everyone and everything in our lives can profoundly transform the living experience.

CHAPTER 1:

Watch Your Language

I think that, in a way, the opening paragraph of a book is the most powerful part, because it essentially determines whether the reader will be interested enough to continue. If this book had begun with a convoluted run-on sentence, reporting dry scientific facts or statistics, do you think you would still be reading this now? Reading a book is an act of choosing the words, thoughts, and ideas you want to have hanging out in your brain for the time being. It is a great privilege and responsibility for a writer to have her words read because it is, in a sense, to be invited into the minds of others. I take this task seriously and hope and pray that these words and ideas make it worth your while.

Do you ever think about the power of words? The role they play in our lives? In our relationships? In our work and our play? The sheer number and diversity of them? The effects and feelings they create? There are almost infinite ways of categorizing words, but for the purpose of this book, I will focus on one particular grouping. The words, sentences, and thoughts we construct can be analyzed much the way we think about behavior, speech, and other areas of function: **counterproductive, neutral, or helpful**. Notice I didn't say "positive" or "negative," because that's not the same thing—but more on that later. To be sure, there is a whole lot of gray area, and we will discuss that as well. But since my primary goal is to present ideas which will enhance your quality of life, I will limit myself to the general applications most relevant to that goal (though I love words so much that I could easily go on and on).

There is a cute graphic making its way around the internet, which has crossed my path several times. In case you missed it, here it is:

Before you speak, THINK:

⇒ Is it **T**rue?
⇒ Is it **H**elpful?
⇒ Is it **I**nspiring?
⇒ Is it **N**ecessary?
⇒ Is it **K**ind?

No doubt, there are times when difficult or painful topics, words, and actions must be confronted, said or done. But, even (and especially) these moments and interactions deserve thought and care so that they may be carried out in the most productive way given the circumstances. They will not always be positive, but they could always be the best possible version of the truth at hand.

More than ten years ago, my husband received a scary diagnosis. It was shocking for an otherwise healthy 32-year-old man to find a Stage 3 tumor in his stomach. We had three children and one on the way when we found out. He is doing really well now, but it was a rough ride for almost two years. I remember the medical professionals who were tactful and caring in their interactions with us. And I remember the ones who were blunt, abrupt or gruff. The communication style dramatically impacted our experience, at times for the better, other times for worse.

Picture, for example, a doctor in the unenviable position of relaying a difficult diagnosis to a patient. This is not good news by any estimation. Let us consider the possible ways of handling the situation through the lens of the three options. They could look something like the following:

Counterproductive: "Well, I've just read all your tests and numbers, and I gotta tell you, it's bad. We must get you in for treatment immediately, but, you know, the prognosis is not good." While this may be accurate information, it's being phrased in a way that is insensitive and even hopeless.

Neutral: "I've just looked at your charts, and it seems you tested positive. We should start treatment as soon as possible because this is a serious condition."

This approach is a bit less terrifying than the one above, and the doctor would have technically done the job of relaying the diagnosis, but now take a look at the third option:

Helpful: "Hi, Mr. and Mrs. Liss. Thanks for coming in today. We received the results from your tests, and unfortunately, they're not what we'd hoped for. It's a serious condition, and we need to treat it aggressively and as soon as we can. There are a number of treatment options, which we can explore together, and while there are no guarantees, our medical team here is committed to doing whatever we can to try for the best possible outcome. I know this is a lot to absorb, so we offer some reading materials to help you understand what we're dealing with and what you can expect. Take some time, look it over, and we'll be here to answer any questions you may have at any point along the way."

Notice how in all three cases, the doctor has conveyed the difficult news, and in each case the news is the same. But as you read through each version, did you feel a difference in the manner and tone? If you did, that is exactly what we're trying to accomplish.

On a lighter note, let's talk about the weather:

The weather is a great example of a reality which generally doesn't have much of an inherent value judgment associated with it. I personally love when it's 87 degrees and sunny out, while most others are baking those days, and running for AC cover. But when I see snow out the window, my heart drops at the thought of frozen sidewalks, dry lips, shoveling the car out, and layers of winter gear. My daughter sees the same snow and squeals in delight—calling the school hotline for cancellations, she pictures snowball fights, snowman contests, sledding, and hot chocolate. The weather is such a powerful and obvious metaphor for mood and internal experience that it is utilized that way in almost every great literary work.

Read the following two descriptions, and note the feelings each one elicits.

Description #1:

"The fierce wind whipped her cheeks pink and raw, and bitter frost clouded her vision and stung her eyes as she plodded through the snowdrifts on feet she could no longer feel."

Not only could we picture the cold itself, but we relate to the pain of experiencing the biting chill through the description.

Now try reading this:

Description #2:

"The snowflakes danced before her eyes, kissed the treetops and gently settled on the earth, a sparkling sheet, flushing cheeks pink and numbing toes as she traipsed home through acres of deep white drifts."

The second sentence also described a girl walking on a cold snowy day. But the mood, tone, and connotations of the words convey joy and beauty, rather than pain and bitterness An author might use the first sentence to depict a woman heading toward something she dreads or away from a harrowing ordeal. She might use the second to create a sense of joyful anticipation or reflective satisfaction. It's all about the tone and context.

Literature will often use the rain as a symbol of cleansing and rebirth, or of mourning and melancholy, depending on the story and type of language used. Likewise, the sun could either be described as harsh, blinding, and blistering, representing punishment or hopelessness, or as warmth, light, wisdom, and healing, representing comfort or hope. All of these examples readily mirror our own individual experiences with the elements and our moods. The weather outside, and the way it's described, could both impact and reflect our internal experience and context. Likewise, we will look at similar factors in our cognitive climate, that flavor our lives and how words shape our thoughts, feelings, moods, and experiences.

There are three primary areas in which we, as Homo sapiens, function in our higher conscious states. These are:

1. **Thought**—what transpires in our heads, our mental processes.

2. **Speech**—what comes out of our mouths, our verbal expression.

3. **Action**—what we do with our physical bodies, our physical communication.

Nearly everything we do when we engage with the world or ourselves exists in one of these three realms. (Ok, yeah, take a minute to think of exceptions, I'll wait...)

These three functions shape who, how, and what we are, and the three are deeply intertwined. For example, all speech has to be on some level "pre-thought" and formulated. And our behaviors then further impact what we think about and discuss. The Horizon of Healthy Function exercise that we explore in this book can be applied to all three modalities, and, where possible, I will try to provide examples in each.

Positive vs. Healthy

Sorry, but I have a bone to pick with positivity. While most of the time, it's probably a good idea to try and stay positive, there are moments and situations when this is inadvisable and even harmful. Imagine that a friend confides in you that she just lost a pregnancy. This is her third miscarriage in a row. You are a fervent believer in positivity, and so you whip out your trusty sunshine and reply, "Well, on the bright side, you know getting pregnant isn't a problem for you." See where positivity can get us into trouble?

While (I hope) it's obvious that this is a supremely insensitive response to another's pain, and most of us know, either intuitively or from experience, not to do this to a friend, we often do this on a more subtle level, both to others and to ourselves. Plants need sunlight, and plenty of it. But a plant that gets only harsh, parching sun and insufficient rainwater will dry up and wither. Positivity is an important ingredient for purposeful living, but it can be overused to the point of detriment. This is why I prefer to substitute "healthy" for "positive." There won't always be an appropriate positive response to every situation, but there is always a healthy option. Positive sometimes denies reality, while healthy accepts it but tries to address, empathize, and/or grow with it.

If debilitating negativity is *below* the Horizon, factual acknowledgement is *on* the Horizon, and excessive positivity is phony and insincere, what we're aiming for is healthy processing—*above* the Horizon, but not so high that you can't see reality. In some examples throughout the book, I will list the "too high" version of thinking, along with the other three. The horizon of health exercise is an approach that honors the feeling or situation as it is without trying to sugarcoat, exacerbate, or deny it. It utilizes words to create a reasonably helpful, hopeful, or accepting tone. Much of this is about word choice.

Two Healthy Options: Acceptance and Action

Have you ever heard the weel-known Serenity Prayer? It goes like this:

"God grant me the serenity
To accept the things I cannot change;

Courage to change the things I can;
And wisdom to know the difference."

This prayer is attributed to the American theologian Reinhold Niebuhr (1892-1971), but has gained wide recognition through the 12-Step addiction treatment model. I don't treat addictions, but I have this prayer hanging on the wall of my office because the idea resonates so much with me, and is applicable to most people and situations. It expresses the reality that there are essentially two possible healthy reactions to a challenge: acceptance and action.

When I sit down with a new client and we try to establish therapeutic goals, one of the first questions I ask myself is: Is this work primarily going to focus on acceptance or action? Usually there is an element of each, but there is generally an emphasis on one or the other. When the reality "is what it is," then the work is generally internal—trying to achieve a feeling of acceptance, harmony, and peace around that reality. On the other hand, when there is a challenge that requires effort to overcome, then we are looking for a plan of action. With the Horizon of Healthy Function technique, we can often utilize one or the other, depending on the person and situation.

Case Study: Avi

Avi is frustrated with his landlords, who live in the unit above him, and make things very difficult for him and his family. They make a lot of noise late at night, leave his mail carelessly scattered on the front stoop, and procrastinate fixing problems that are technically their job to fix. Avi's wife is more relaxed about it, choosing instead to appreciate the unusually low rent they pay for this subpar arrangement. I ask Avi what he would like to do: Would he like to strategize about finding another place to live or learn coping skills for dealing with this undesirable set up? He tells me that they've asked around, and if they want to remain in the area, they will not find a comparable rental that is this affordable, and they can't pay more at this time.

His therapeutic reframing, or narrative *edit*, ended up looking something like this:

1. *Below* **the Horizon:** "I hate those stupid neighbors—they have no respect for us, they are awful people, and I don't even care that I will probably break a hole in the ceiling from all the broom-pounding I do trying to shut them up. I hate that we're stuck in this crummy apartment."

2. *On* **the Horizon:** "This situation is really frustrating. They are difficult neighbors, and besides that, they are our landlords and they really don't seem interested   in accommodating our needs at all, but we can't afford to move."

3. *Above* **the Horizon:** "It stinks to live with people like this, and the minute we can consider another option, we will. But for now, we will try to view their tactlessness as part of the price we pay for getting such a reasonable deal on this living

space. We will continue to calmly voice our complaints and requests, but with the recognition that it probably won't help much. In the meantime, we will try to save a little bit monthly so we can eventually afford a better home."

See how the edit primarily includes an element of accepting the less-than-ideal situation for what it is and also adds a bit of hope for being able to take small action towards the future? These are the two parts of the Serenity Prayer: acceptance and action. Often, once there is some aspect of acceptance, mental energy that was previously wasted on getting upset can be redirected toward proactive steps, which is exactly what happened in this case. About a year later, Avi and his family were able to upgrade to a better apartment in a nice building.

Calibrating Language

When my husband and I were newlyweds, he started feeling very lethargic, and he was diagnosed with mono. It was very interesting to see how differently people reacted when we shared this with them. Here are some of the types of responses I noticed:

1. **Catastrophizing**: "Oh, man! Mono is the worst! It lasts for ages and you feel like you can't move… and it's really dangerous if you get pregnant… you must be so upset!"

2. **Dismissive/self-absorbed**: "That's annoying. You know, my cousin had mono once, and I think she had to take a semester off grad school. Actually, she recently moved to Canada."

3. **Matter-of-fact:** "Mono, huh? That's the one where you're very tired all the time, right?"

4. **Silver lining:** "Well, at least he's not in pain, and it's not, like, dangerous. You just wait it out, right? And, like, you can use this time to really bond and get closer."

5. **Empathetic**: "Wow—that sounds hard. Is he ok? Does he need medication? Is there anything we can do to help? I hope he feels better soon."

Of course, you can share the same news with twelve different friends and you'll get twelve different reactions. But the words and tones we use to weave our interactions make a big difference in where they take us.

Negative experiences and emotions have a significant role in the human condition. To try and elbow them out of our consciousness entirely is to reject reality and miss opportunities for personal growth. Negativity in and of itself is not the problem; it's *unproductive* negativity that gets us into trouble.

For example, anger is not inherently a positive or pleasant emotion, yet it's something worth limiting most of the time. But a form of productive anger, like righteous indignation that leads to fighting evil, righting societal wrongs, and idealistic activism, is a vital instrument of human progress. Likewise, if we are dealing with loss, sadness is a healthy and appropriate feeling. In a moment of danger, the adrenaline that fear generates can help us find safety. And to feign positivity, in the case of the miscarriage of justice or in the face of danger, is not only unhealthy, but counterproductive.

So for our purposes, we are discussing how to deal with and diminish *unproductive* negative emotion, not all negative emotion.

Sometimes, I'll have a client who is struggling with anxiety. One of the techniques we'll use is what we call "calibrating descriptives." I'll ask her to list, for example, seven different synonyms for the feeling of anxiety, of varying levels of intensity, and then to rate them from strongest to weakest. One woman came up with the following:

- freaking out
- terrified
- panicky
- very anxious
- stressed
- worried
- concerned

We'll write each one down on an index card, and then practice deep breathing as she reads between each one. When she feels a panic attack building, she can take out her cards. She takes a breath, looks at the first one, exhales, and says, "Ok, I feel like I'm freaking out." Then she takes 3 deep breaths and flips to the next card to read: "Ok, I still feel terrified." Three more breaths, and the next card: "Feeling panicky." More breathing followed by, "I'm very anxious." You see where this is going. "I'm stressed, scared, worried, concerned, uneasy…"

By slowly, deliberately breathing her way down the spectrum of emotional intensity, she is able to accept the general state she is in, but also to assume some control over the manner and the intensity with which she feels the feelings. By the end of the simple exercise, she may still feel concerned, but "concerned" is a manageable emotion and can usually be easily tolerated or addressed, while "freaking out" is overwhelming and unproductive. (Like all therapeutic techniques, this has limitations. There is a time and a place, and it will not work 100% of the time. Sometimes it takes a few tries, and sometimes it won't help at all. But often it does, and it can be a valuable tool.)

Another example of calibrating negative affect into manageability could be used regarding depression:

- totally devastated
- utterly despondent
- feeling despair
- very discouraged
- disappointed
- somewhat down
- a little sad

By simply, slowly, and mindfully breathing through and feeling the words from intense to mild, a person can shift her consciousness toward where she wants to be.

Even outside of therapy, the idea of utilizing nuances in language can be extremely powerful. Imagine using the following internal shift in thought process.

1. *Below* **the Horizon:** "Boy, do I hate my job! My boss is so unreasonable, my coworkers are lazy, and I just wish I were anywhere else."

You stew in your own resentment for a few moments, and then the guy in the next cubicle brings you some coffee, exactly how you like it. Your mood softens, and suddenly your thinking changes to something more like:.

2. *On* **the Horizon:** "Eh, I was really just having a bad day. It's true, the boss can be difficult, and not everyone pulls their weight here. Of course I'd rather be on a beach, but most days I really don't mind what I do, and this is a pretty decent place to work."

Often, there is more than one true version of reality. Even if the first version was more accurate, it could be edited to something more helpful.

3. *Above* **the Horizon:** "I'm noticing that I don't get much satisfaction from my job. I find it hard to work for this employer, and it seems that others

do too. It pays the bills for now, but maybe I should think about trying to look for a new job at some point."

Reversing the "But" Statement

I'd like to invite you into my brain for a moment. (I'm not sure who should be more apprehensive about that—you or me.) I'd like to show you an example of how this book almost didn't get completed and then why it did. Please take a moment to read each of the two sentences below slowly and carefully, and then note the similarities and differences between them:

Sentence #1:

> *"I know I really want to prioritize writing a piece about improving healthy functioning, **but** I have so many started projects in my Word document files that I get overwhelmed at the very thought of narrowing them down and actually committing to finishing one of them."*

Sentence #2:

> *"I have so many started projects in my Word document files that I get overwhelmed at the very thought of narrowing them down and actually committing to finishing one of them, but I know I really want to prioritize writing a piece about improving healthy functioning."*

Were you able to find the similarities and differences? Word for word, the sentences are almost identical. Each one has a statement followed by the word "but" and then another statement. Each one expresses the idea of wanting to write a book on healthy functioning and also the idea of being overwhelmed at the work involved. Yet, in sentence #1, the goal is stated first, with the "but" presenting an obstacle that leaves the reader with a sense that perhaps this will be too difficult. The inferable conclusion from sentence #1 is something like: "I have this nice idea, but it's not going to happen."

In sentence #2, the obstacle is presented first, and the word "but" is followed by an assertion that I very much would like to achieve the goal anyway. The inferable conclusion from sentence #2 is more like: "This isn't going to be easy, but it's important to me, so I'd like to try."

Each sentence reflects both the goal and the obstacle, but changing the structure from sentence #1 to sentence #2 changes not only the order, but the very meaning of the thought being expressed. Looking at it more analytically, sentence #1 is a wish with a limitation and doubt, while sentence #2 is an acknowledgement of difficulty with a choice to make an attempt. Shifting from "sentence #1 thinking" to "sentence #2 thinking" is something I often practice with my clients, and I call it "reversing the 'but' statement" (and yes, my children chuckle when I say this).

"Reversing the 'but' statement" is a technique that works with couples as well as in our own individual thoughts.

Case Study: Lisa and Dave

Lisa and Dave came to marital therapy on the brink of divorce. They had just moved back in together after a trial separation, wanting to give the marriage another shot "for the sake of the kids." Of the many issues with which they struggled, one of them was Lisa's chronic negative feelings about how Dave spent his time. To be sure, they each had areas to work on in the marriage, and we did couple sessions as well as individual, or "solo," ones, but here I'd like to share with you a segment of one of Lisa's "solo" sessions:

> **Lisa**: Dave is great with the kids, and he's helpful around the house. But I really had hoped he'd get more involved in the community, in outreach, in growing his career. He just always stays home instead of going out there and making something of himself. It's hard to respect him.

> **Me**: I can hear your frustration; you wish he were more proactive, ambitious, idealistic. We can discuss that further in a together session and see how he feels about that. In the meantime, would you like to try and push him harder, or would you like to work on being able to accept him for now and enjoy his

good qualities? *[Note: Here am I trying to help Lisa determine whether we want to be moving toward action or acceptance.]*

Lisa: Oh, I've already tried pushing him hard, and I know that never ends well. I wish I could just accept and enjoy his better qualities. But I just always end up noticing and thinking about what he doesn't do, and it gets me feeling all down about him and us as a couple. *[So she is seeking acceptance.]*

Me: Let's try this. The way we think influences the way we feel. So, it follows that if we can edit our thoughts to be healthier, we can impact how we feel in a positive way. *[I then explain the idea of "reversing the 'but' statement."]* So now, you're thinking:

"Dave is great with the kids and housework, but it annoys me that he's pretty unambitious and not proactive in the community."

You catch yourself thinking that thought and know from experience that it will only result in your feeling judgmental, resentful, frustrated, and sorry for yourself. Instead of going down that old familiar ugly road, you can remind yourself that by slightly editing the thought— without changing the truth or ignoring any information—it could look and feel very different.

Instead of, "Dave is great with the kids and housework, but it annoys me that he's unambitious and not proactive in the community," think:

"It bothers me that Dave is not so ambitious or proactive, BUT he really is great with the kids and helpful around the house."

It's the same information, but by just reversing the parts of the sentence, you create a very different feeling for yourself. The situation is still not perfect, but it's more hopeful, more acceptable for the meantime, somehow. This way, you honor and acknowledge the area where you are troubled, but you refocus your perspective and emphasize what you can enjoy for now. Does that sound like it's worth a try?

Lisa: It makes sense logically and sounds simple… Does it really work?

Me: Why don't you try it out for yourself and see. Write down either the two versions of the statements that we just used or any other example. Then read them each out loud and tell me if you feel a difference. But remember, both sentences must be true to your experience.

Lisa tried this exercise and then applied the idea to a few other toxic thoughts that tended to recur in her mind. She was a bit skeptical, but open to exploring it further. I asked her to journal some more examples during the week and see whether or not she found it helpful. While it certainly didn't solve all of their problems (nor was it supposed to), it gave Lisa a valuable tool for when she found herself spiraling into a rut of negative thinking, and she was able to challenge and edit those thoughts for the better. This helped her to keep her mood and attitude better at times when it would have otherwise gone downhill from a small observation.

Please note: For this technique to be effective, the two clauses must be somewhat comparable. "My husband may be an axe murderer, but at least he has pretty eyes" won't be as helpful.

A Brief Description of Narrative Therapy and Why I Love It

When I was in grad school, we studied a number of different approaches to therapy. Some were more classical, like Freud's psychoanalysis, and others more contemporary, such as Sue Johnson's emotionally focused therapy. As students, we each dutifully memorized terms and applied concepts while researching papers and studying for exams, and then played around with them to find our callings.

I found myself gravitating toward a relatively obscure approach called "Narrative Therapy." The narrative approach to therapy was established by Michael White and David Epston of the Dulwich Center in Australia. It's based on the idea that each of us is living our own story. Therefore, in a very observable way, our reality and perspectives are created by words. Our knowledge of nouns—people, places, things, concepts, our relationships, our sense of self, our memories, our goals, our thoughts—are all comprised of the same basic building blocks: words.

In ancient Biblical Hebrew, the word *"davar"* is used to mean "word," "object," and "leader." This is explained by the fact that words have power, influence, existence, and reality—much as concrete objects and rulers do. We tend to think our thoughts in involuntary trains from a very young age, accumulating more varied and sophisticated vocabulary as we mature and learn. We label, analyze, assess, and relate to our surroundings through the language that lives organically in our minds and express ourselves using those same words.

Jean Piaget, a staple thinker for any Psychology 101 course, applied the terms assimilation and accommodation to the process of using language to assign meaning to experience. Assimilation is when children fit the experience into whatever vocabulary they already have. Accommodation is when they need to learn new words, to make space in their consciousness for new discoveries, and thereby expand their worlds.

A toddler, for example, may only know of the word "doggy" as a reference for "animal." She may be taken to visit a zoo and will emphatically point to each four-legged, furry mammal and yell, "Doggy! Doggy!" because that is her frame of reference. An older child with more knowledge and vocabulary to distinguish between the animals will be more likely to appreciate the diversity of wildlife, and a zoologist will have exponentially more appreciation for the nuances of the various species. Likewise, as citizens of the world, the more insight and lexicon we collect, the more we can make discernments and the more broadly and deeply we observe, analyze, and connect with our experiences.

The goal of narrative therapy is to capitalize on the fact that we construct our perceptions,— and hence our realities,— using the medium of words. We claim ownership of our **narratives** and invite our clients to do the same—assuming the full right and privilege to become the authors of our life stories. We're not always in control of the external *plot* (more about that later), but often we have more power than we realize, and we can also choose how to frame and relate to it all. We can introduce descriptives, subtleties, and connotations to create feeling and meaning around experience.

Here's a personal example. When I was applying to colleges, I was a smart-mouthed, outspoken, opinionated high school senior. On one memorable interview, I was asked why I wanted to attend that particular university. Without giving much thought to my answer, I replied, way too honestly, "To tell you the truth, I've never been a big fan of institutionalized education. I prefer autodidactic learning, and I always have. But I realize that to get most jobs one needs a degree of higher learning, and I like the wide selection of courses you offer. So I might as well attend classes in subjects I enjoy." While most would argue that I wasn't using great judgment in answering the question this way, I often marvel at how little my feelings have changed over the past two decades. I still have a strong resistance to educational establishments.

And so, I've always had mixed feelings about sending my children to school. In retrospect, part of me wishes we had homeschooled them. This is not the place for an essay on the pros and cons of each option, but during the times we were less than enamored with our choice to school them traditionally, or the schools they were in, I found myself thinking thoughts such as the following.

1. *Below* **the Horizon:** "Who decided that children were meant to be mass-produced? Are we aiming to create robots, clones, to passively absorb predigested bytes of dry data, or to nurture individual souls and gifts? Schools just kill the joy of learning! How is this experience squelching my children's potential…?"

Now while these rhetorical questions might have some merit in a discussion seriously addressing the pros and cons of various educational options, once the kids were in school, all this did was put me in a state of distress over the drawbacks of the system we'd chosen. After a while, I trained myself to edit the thought as follows. I began by simply acknowledging my doubts and frustrations.

2. ***On* the Horizon:** "I often wonder about schooling as the primary modality for educating kids. I tend to see so many flaws in the traditional systems, and find myself mentally exploring alternative methods such as homeschooling. When I feel this way after a particularly unpleasant interaction with a school, I realize I'm being mostly reactive. But when I think about it from a calm and rational perspective, perhaps it's something to consider for the future."

From the place of less intense emotionality, and a bit more objectivity and balance, I was then able to formulate the following option.

3. ***Above* the Horizon:** "Sometimes I question whether in fact I want my children educated in this manner. And if my husband and I want to revisit this discussion seriously, we should schedule a time to pour some coffee and do so. But for now, I will focus on the benefits of having them in a conventional school environment. Since no system is perfect, when problems arise, we will sincerely try to address them in a calm and realistic way. And if we eventually choose to sit down, make a pros-cons list, and go in a different direction with the family, we know that's always a legitimate possibility, too."

Note: Since the writing of the above segment, we have indeed begun homeschooling some of our children, as per their interests, and have found it thus far to be quite rewarding all around.

I never made a conscious decision to become a narrative therapist; I prefer to view my practice approach as more "collaborative" and "integrative". Collaborative means that my first priority is to hear what the clients want to accomplish and join them in formulating and strategizing their goals; that is my only agenda. Integrative, in that I try to use helpful and relevant research, techniques, and concepts from diverse sources in treating each client or couple. Yet, somehow, all things being equal, I find myself magnetically pulled toward narrative ideology and application. The idea of our lives as stories resonates deeply with my soul and style. I like to think of myself as an author, with the *authority* (see that word root thing again?) to script the narration to suit my values, beliefs, moods, and desire. I like the power of knowing that while I can't control everything, I get to write the book, or at least my own evolving *mental memoir*, about how it's all portrayed. And we all know: the pen is mightier than the sword. (Which isn't really true if you're trying to stab someone. Probably, I assume. I never tried. Promise.)

For my clients, too, so much of their experience—emotional, cognitive, relational—resides in language. By visiting, tasting, seasoning, editing, and redecorating the words that circulate between our minds, hearts, and souls, we can change our internal realities, or even create entirely new and better versions. This, in turn, can then impact the external experience. It may sound too simple or good to be true, and sometimes it is. But it's also elegant, profound, powerful, and often extremely effective.

CHAPTER 2:

Starting With the Self

By now you're probably getting the picture of how this exercise works theoretically, but the best (and most interesting) way to illustrate it is by using examples. Most of us tend to think about pretty much everything in our lives. So there's no shortage of material if we want to practice the skill of improving our thought processes. We could begin anywhere, really, but let's work from the inside out. By enhancing the way we relate to ourselves, it will become easier to find healthier ways to relate to everything else.

In general, narratives tend to be more interesting, instructive, and memorable than theories. (See, wasn't that a boring sentence? That's because it was a theory.) So let's take a look at a narrative and then we can extrapolate some principles.

The following true story (with pseudonyms and changes for privacy) was taken from one of the many Word documents that I had never published:

Case Study: Shari's Narrative Paradigm Shift Moment

Although she's just shy of five feet even in her wedges, Shari walked into her 10 a.m. session standing a little taller than usual. We'd been working together for almost four months. An agreeable, intelligent woman(a professor, actually), she always seemed to absorb my suggestions, but I was often not sure how much they were helping her. She had originally presented with mild dysthymia, a long-term depressive disorder, but in our time together navigated a marital crisis, and revisited some personal history.

But on that Wednesday morning, she looked decidedly different. She sported a brightly colored ensemble with coordinating handbag, while a chunky gem necklace smiled around her collar, but paled beneath her eyes.

"I've finally turned my corner!" she reported. I settled back into my chair for the story. What was so touching to me about it was how ostensibly ordinary it was. A simple, slice-of-life vignette.

But first, a little background:

Shari's mom was the eldest daughter of Holocaust survivors. Her grandparents were traumatized, scarred, and unforgiving, and her mother became harsh and depressed. Growing up, Shari and her siblings learned to do everything quietly and well, but also learned that regardless of their efforts, they would be criticized. As an adult, Shari continued to push herself hard, judge herself rigidly, and eschew taking credit. She tried to be loving to her own children, but found it felt hollow and fake. She had a good job where she was well-respected, but berated herself disproportionately for any imperfections, objective or perceived.

We had been trying to rescript her inner narrative, replacing self- judgments and recrimination with compassion and introspective serenity. We were trying to reprogram her instincts away from self- loathing and avoidance and toward self-acceptance and gentle growth. Intellectually astute, she embraced the concepts, but emotionally deprived, had difficulty applying them.

On that Wednesday she knew: By George, she's got it! She and her family had spent a long weekend out of town reconnecting with an old friend. Her friend was the same age as she; in fact,, they'd been classmates. They had similar lives, both married with three young kids, similar jobs, homes, incomes, and backgrounds. But Shari noticed an important difference. She saw that even though their kids were the same ages and their homes similar in size, her friend Riki's home seemed to run more smoothly and efficiently. It was set up in a more user-friendly way, more organized and logical. The children were trained with specific tasks, were more capable and helpful, and had more structured activities than in Shari's home.

So why was Shari so happy? In the past, a weekend like this would have been very painful for her. Her mind would have been filled with thoughts of inferiority and shame, such as, "Riki's got it together, and I'm all over the place… I have no excuse; we have the same life but she's doing it well and I'm drowning… I can't do anything right… Maybe she should raise my kids for me… I don't want her to ever see my house after this… I'm just a loser…"

Instead, she had a wonderful stay. The whole time, she was observing Riki's family and routine, complimenting her friend on what a great job she was doing with her family and home. She found herself being inspired and uplifted and able to learn from her friend. She was thinking much more productive thoughts like, "Wow, Riki really has a great system in place, and her life situation is very similar to mine. There's no reason why I can't implement a lot of these ideas and enjoy the same benefits. I'm really happy to be able to get a front row seat at this live efficiency seminar. I'm catching up with an old friend and learning some great parenting and homemaking tips all at once."

She confided in Riki that she struggles in these areas and asked a lot of questions about how Riki handles the details of her home, kids, and job. Riki was flattered and thrilled to share. They enjoyed a delightful weekend together and later followed up by phone.

Shari was especially proud of herself because when we began working together, she would have only seen the bleak comparison, focused on her inferiority, and retreated into hopeless shame and discouragement. First, we worked on creating alternate, helpful responses to life situations in our sessions. Eventually, she learned to do it on her own in her journal at the end of the day. Finally, she began to reframe her thinking even as the events were occurring in real time. But the reason for her joy this time was that this productive way of thinking (or *above* the Horizon of Healthy Thinking, which generated healthier functioning) had finally become second nature to her. She had not only learned the skill, but internalized the habit. It was at that session we determined she was ready to move therapy to an "as needed" basis.

If we break down Shari's story into the Horizon exercise, it looks something like this:

1. *Below* **the Horizon:** "Riki is capable and creative, while I am incompetent and sloppy. Her home and family are so well tended that it reminds me what a lousy job I'm doing with mine. I really stink at this stuff."

2. *On* **the Horizon:** "I see that Riki runs her home and family life very efficiently, especially when I compare it to my own. She seems to have more of a knack for the maternal/domestic than I do."

3. *Above* **the Horizon:** "Watching Riki's homemaking and parenting shows me that there are a lot of great ideas she uses that maybe I can learn from. It's a bit humbling to see how much better she is at this than I am, but spending time

with her, observing her, and discussing it with her will allow me to pick up some tips and habits that could really enhance my home."

It may sound like a small deal, but it can make a tremendous difference in quality of life.

Jealousy vs. Learning From Other People: A Matter of Horizon

Several years ago, I was teaching a course in a local college. We were analyzing a text, and we realized something profound: "The only difference between jealousy and learning from others is mood." When I'm in a good mood and I see someone being/doing/having something I wish I were being/doing/having, I can feel inspired and uplifted to emulate whatever that thing is. But when I'm feeling down—on myself, about that other person, or about life in general—and I am exposed to that same stimulus of someone else being/doing/having something I want, I can end up feeling jealous or resentful of that person, or self-critical and depressed. It's the same input, with alternate processes.

Betty spent a few weeks being jealous of her new neighbor's front garden. Sometimes she judged the Johnsons as being showy for having such bold landscaping, and other times she just compared and felt bad about her overgrown hedges and crabgrass. It was only after a particularly potent espresso one Sunday morning, that she was struck with the inspiration to compliment Sheila on her flowers, and ask for the number of their gardener. A lovely friendship ensued, along with an upgraded garden.

My youngest daughter, Ahuva, shared something very sensitive with me this morning: "Sometimes, I want to tell you about something really nice or fun I did with one of my sisters. Like last night, we were up late talking and laughing and it was so much fun. But I feel bad, because you don't have any sisters, and I don't want to make you sad."

I was touched by her thoughtfulness, and I tried to explain. "Thank you so much for thinking about my feelings. But I love hearing about you enjoying your sisters; I wish I had sisters too, but the fact that you enjoy yours just makes me proud and happy for you that you have each other and that I have you guys, too."

She smiled and said, "That's a happier way to look at it." A young lesson in Horizon thinking.

It isn't only comparisons with others that generate this sort of self talk. The first relationship we have is with ourselves. Babies are not born with self-esteem issues; they tend to be pretty matter-of- fact and assertive about their needs. As we develop, though, we tend to internalize assessments about who and what we are, can, or should be. Some of these labels are very helpful. If we are fortunate, we become aware of our natural strengths, interests, and challenges. We are taught by the adults in our lives to try and be kind, considerate, compassionate, generous, thoughtful, hard- working, creative, and curious, and these qualities are rewarded and reinforced.

But loving people are, unfortunately, not the only or even the most influential voices in our development. Hypercriticism and cruelty from other children and adults as we develop can sometimes chip away at our confidence and self-image, creating shame and doubt, and take root in our own minds.

Imagine a world in which children received only loving, encouraging, gentle, constructive feedback from those around them. Wouldn't that be beautiful? Now try and recreate your own internal self-image based on what that would have been like for you. It's not too late, even if you received a great deal of critical or cruel messages about yourself growing up. You have the power to rewrite your internal assessment, right here, right now.

Here's an easy exercise. Imagine you had a child with your exact makeup—genetically, behaviorally, the whole package. You love this child with all your heart, and you are put in charge of loving and nurturing that child— her strengths, her challenges, her behaviors. What would you say? What would you do? How would you describe her, to her or to others? If you can, and you're ready, really take a moment to think about how you would do this. So often, we get caught up in some unhealthy distortion of humility, where we don't want to see or acknowledge even the obvious goodness in ourselves. When I hear clients being gratuitously hard on or unforgiving of themselves, I often ask them the following question: "What would you say to a friend who was saying these things about herself?" This is generally followed by either a sincere reassurance, or a sheepish smile.

In relationships, we often struggle with being "above" or "below." Take a moment to think about the different people in your life. Many of our relationships are naturally hierarchical, meaning someone has more power. A parent, older sibling, teacher, employer, or practitioner is usually cast as "above." A child, younger sibling, student, employee, or patient is, in a sense, "below." Even with our peers, sometimes we feel equally "in" with the other, while at other times, we may feel we are doing the other a favor by making time for them, or vice versa. In love relationships, we call this dynamic the "pursuer-distancer." In any kind of connection, there can be a feeling of one party being more invested than the other.

A wonderful feeling within a relationship is when we are at emotional eye level with the other. It's that sense of: I get, respect, admire, and care about you, and you do the same for me. We're not evaluating, judging, competing, or comparing; we're just interacting as two accepting equals. We don't feel better than or less than; we just "are." When we have that with a friend or a colleague, it's a great feeling. If we can get that way with ourselves, all the better. That's a big deal- being able to view ourselves without diminishing or embellishing any of our parts. Imagine being able to look in the mirror (physically and metaphorically) and just comfortably say, "Oh yeah, that's me." (Or "that is I," for the pathologically grammatical.)

That is Horizon thinking, vis-à-vis ourselves: looking ourselves straight in the face, without magnifying every flaw or smearing goopy cover-up all over it, just gently holding the gaze and saying, "Hi there. Nice to see you."

Let's take a look at some personal traits and qualities and the various lenses through which we tend to interpret them.

Introversion: Many introverts get misunderstood and misinterpreted. When you don't talk much, others can more easily jump to conclusions or put words in your mouth. It's easy to buy into that. Introverts are often labeled as shy, quiet, reserved, anxious, nerdy, insecure, dumb, weak, snobby, antisocial, boring, or aloof. When an introvert hears that enough times, he may internalize those feelings or identify with them.

On the flipside, a healthy, self-assured introvert could view himself as pensive, thoughtful, prudent, refined, gentle, a good listener, respectful, and easy on the nerves. (Susan Cain wrote a terrific book on the subject called *Quiet: The Power of Introverts in a World that Can't Stop Talking*.)

Extroversion: If you like to express yourself to others and enjoy their company, you might be an extrovert.

I personally could never tell whether I was an extrovert or an introvert because I love interacting with people, teaching, running groups, counseling, and focused socializing, but I dislike small talk, parties, weddings, concerts, and other large, loud, social gatherings. I also really love and need my alone time. One of my clients taught me the word "centrovert," which made me super happy, because it validated my intuition that I am indeed both. Are you? When I am in my extroverted mindset, I tend to worry that I am attention-seeking, showing off, interrupting, and/or monopolizing the conversation. Indeed, this is the occupational hazard of the extrovert, and I'm sure I have been guilty of all of the above. I used to quip to my students that teaching was my functional way of hogging the spotlight.

But here's the funny thing: When I see public speakers whom I respect doing their public speaking thing, I generally don't condemn them this way. I'll think thoughts like, "He really knows how to engage the crowd," or, "I love how she weaves spontaneous humor into her purposeful message." After my lectures, friends and attendees often approach me with similarly warm feedback, along with comments like, "You seem so comfortable in front of a mic; I would get really nervous." I try to internalize the useful responses as encouragement and to deflect the superlative ones as outliers.

A couple of months ago, I had an unusual experience in which I gave a lecture in another state and afterwards was sent my "ratings," as solicited by the host organization, from the audience.

Most of the comments were positive and kind, the praise specific, and the critique constructive, but there were a couple of extreme ones: "I thought she was absolutely amazing!!" and "She was horrible and all over the place." It was unsettling to be privy to these people's responses, but shortly afterwards, I was listening to Dennis Prager on the radio, and he said something very wise, as he often does. He said that in order to keep a balanced perspective on his work, he doesn't put too much stock in extreme compliments or criticism. If he hears a critique or praise that is useful, in that it helps him to improve his show by correcting flaws or enhancing his strengths, then he happily accepts and utilizes it. But he doesn't let hurtful insults get to his heart or excessive admiration get to his head. As a public figure for over 30 years, this policy seems to have stood him in good stead, and was exactly what I needed to hear after this strange interaction.

I realized that it's not only the feelings and opinions of others that need to be taken with a grain of salt, but our own as well. We can be our own harshest critics and our own false advertisers. When we're able to refrain from beating ourselves up or over-inflating our images, we're left with the honest, simple facts. Those are the best criteria for self-assessment. In this case, when I stripped away the sense of flattery I felt from the superlative reviews and the pang of hurt I felt reading the harsh one, I was able to analyze my presentation more objectively. I determined that I had taught useful material and presented in a relatable way, but that it could be better organized into a cleaner handout for future clarity.

Self-recrimination is one way we wax unhealthy in relationship to ourselves. The other extreme can take us to unhealthy places, too, even if not technically *below* the Horizon. I have an acquaintance who made a nice amount of money through a network marketing company. At first, her contagious enthusiasm was endearing. But then it started to get a little evangelical and aggressive. She would regularly share with anyone she could access via social media and real life how many goals she was hitting, how many promotions she was earning, how many converts she was accruing. Then she shifted to mocking anyone who didn't want to join the business, who opted for a conventional job and paycheck, while she was "sticking it to the world." She developed a grandiose, superior posture that felt uncomfortably pejorative to any of us who were not interested in selling those products.

When she asked me what I thought of her campaign, I told her that I admired her ambition and success, but that I personally preferred some of her earlier posts and shares over the more intense recent ones and explained why. She thought for a moment, and thanked me for the honesty, but then explained that I was probably just resisting "getting outside my comfort zone."

Ok, then. I relate to her defensiveness because I've been there, too. I used to sport annoying arrogance about my own specific abilities and values, and maybe sometimes I still do, when I'm not careful. I've worked for many years at separating healthy confidence from obnoxious pretentiousness. In my particular case, since I believe in G-d, I was able to utilize that construct in this work, but you could substitute "nature," "good fortune," or "the universe," too. Anything I am or have or can do is something that was given to me as a gift. And when I get too cocky about it, I usually need a humbling reminder that "There but for the grace of God, go I."

The spiritual reminder is helpful in both directions. My tradition has a beautiful piece of advice: We should have a proverbial note folded into each of our two pockets. On one should have the Biblical quote from Abraham, "I am but dust and ashes." And the other should read, "For my sake, the world was created." When I am feeling too proud and self-important, I need to remember where I came from, where I'm headed, and from where I received my gifts. And when I'm feeling low and down and worthless, I need to remember that I have an immortal soul, a Divine spirit, and am therefore endowed with greatness, purpose, and potential.

A tale is told of King Solomon, wisest of men. As perhaps the most prosperous of ancient Jewish monarchs from the ripe age of 12, he foresaw potential instability. He requested of his sages that they fashion him a trinket that would both uplift him when he was feeling low and ground him when he was feeling too high. He was presented with a signet ring that had the Hebrew words for the simple epithet, "This too shall pass." When you're feeling down, worried, or discouraged, remember that this will pass and you will feel strong, hopeful, and happy again. When you're feeling complacent, haughty, or prideful about something, remember that this too is a moment; it doesn't make you inherently better than anyone else, and it will be followed by more challenges.

It's a very delicate balance to not see ourselves as "lower than" or "higher than," but simply here, and in most ways, equal to, others. That doesn't mean we're all equal in every way; we are obviously not all equal in physical strength, intellectual ability, talent, or moral goodness. We each have our strengths and challenges. We're not born equally gifted, nor do we strive or achieve in equal measures to each other. But as far as intrinsic value or personhood, we are all simply citizens of the same green planet, trying to do our best to enhance it while we are here.

The first place to start in making the world a better place is, of course, ourselves. When I am kinder, more tolerant, more accepting, more patient, more encouraging of myself, when I see myself as a human being with inherent value and potential, I practice generating goodness from the inside out. When I reject harsh, overstated self-criticism and instead choose to view my own flaws and mistakes with gentle clarity, grace, and hope, I actually increase my likelihood for self-improvement. When I espouse a harmonious mixture of self-love and humility, I can view my strengths and successes as gifts, tools, and tokens, and I hold space for more abundance and endowment going forward.

Some rare, lucky souls seem to cruise through life on emotionally stable autopilot, somehow striking the appropriate feeling for every occasion. They just naturally self-regulate. Those people are very fortunate. Then there are the rest of us, who fluctuate, and need to cultivate self-awareness and work on our reactions and temperaments. As we continue to explore the Horizon of Healthy Thinking, we will look at some tools for doing just that.

CHAPTER 3:

Not That We're Judging, but...

"He's kind of a loser..."

"She's really awkward..." "They're so stupid..."

How many times a day do you hear, say, or think something categorically unkind or dismissive about another person?

A hallmark of contemporary culture is the value, even worship, of diversity, tolerance and acceptance. On the flipside, the tendency to be judgmental and discredit others is viewed with disdain. (See the irony? We are so committed to the value of nonjudgment, that we become very judgmental of those whom we label judgmental.) But the value of trying not to judge others is actually older than we might think. The Bible itself says in Lev. 19: "With righteousness you should judge your people." The Babylonian Talmud, which is the source for an abundance of ancient wisdom, goes a step further: "Don't judge your fellow until you arrive in his place." This means, simply, that if you're not the guy, you can't judge the guy. The human tendency to size each other up seems universal;

even in the animal kingdom, two creatures will generally give one another a once-over to determine whether friend or foe and establish dominance. And to a certain extent, there is a survival instinct involved. If we get a "creepy vibe" from someone following us on a quiet street after dark, we're likely to forget about political correctness, and get ourselves to safety, ASAP.

Most of us probably try to think of ourselves as fair-minded and nonjudgmental. But when it comes down to it, our thoughts and words can sometimes take us to less than savory places. The Horizon of Healthy Thinking concept can be applied to help us enhance our thinking when it comes to relating to others.

I remember years ago shopping in Costco with one of my kids, who was very young at the time, riding in the front of the wagon. She was people-watching our fellow shoppers, and at one point, she pointed to a very heavyset woman and called out, for all to hear, "That lady is so big!"

Disappointed that there was no hole into which I could crawl, I curbed my instinct to call out, "Excuse me, did anyone lose this child?" and tried do some damage control. I wasn't sure the woman had heard her, so I didn't want to call attention to it by apologizing. I decided to at least try to make a learning moment out of it, and once we were safely out of earshot, I sagely parented my progeny, "Saying out loud, 'That lady is so big,' could hurt the lady's feelings. It's better not to comment on the way people look, but if you do want to, we could say nice things, like, 'I like your hair' or 'Your dress is pretty.'" My little one nodded, and seemed to understand. A few aisles later, we passed by a man with long scraggly hair and beard, in tattered clothes, walking a bit erratically. My daughter's eyes widened, but then she looked at him and said, "Your dress is pretty."

Sometimes we just don't know what to say or think, and it feels like the only options are brutal honesty or inauthenticity. The Horizon approach looks at the possibilities between the blunt "That lady is so big" and the absurd "Your dress is pretty."

Many adults have this either/or thinking problem. They'll say: "Well, do you want me to be honest and keep it real or just lie and tell you what you want to hear?" Um, no. I'd like you to be constructive, respectful, appropriate, and kind, please. If you can't be honest without being mean, then kindly zip it.

There are some sanguine souls who can encounter others and not really register much. Their mellow minds mildly muse (pardon my irritating tendency to gratuitously wax alliterative) something like, "Oh look, a fellow Homo sapien, perhaps I'll offer a polite smile and then move right along. Oh look, a tree." Then there are the rest of us with our active imaginations and quick conclusions. I can notice a person walking towards me, and in less than five seconds have instinctively, even involuntarily, concocted an elaborate mental biography for him, complete with personal history, relationships, and favorite sitcom.

With regard to noticing someone's unseemly appearance, here is a sample of intentionally edited thinking:

1.   *Below* **the Horizon** (*often our first instinct*): "Ugh, what an ugly person."

2.   *On* **the Horizon:** "I notice that individual is unattractive."

3.   *Above* **the Horizon:** "I noticed that the first thing I saw about that stranger is his homeliness. I would like to actively shift gears and instead think, that is a human being with a mind, and a heart, and feelings that matter. It's not easy to live in a world where the first thing people see is what meets the eyes, if one is not pleasing to look at. Instead of registering him as an 'ugly guy,' I will make a point to nod or smile, as I would to any other decent company. And remind myself that, of course, it's what's inside that matters."

Sometimes, in our haste to transform a negative thought, we may be tempted to morph it into an opposite, positive thought. If this can be done sincerely, then great, but often it feels inauthentic within the self, and we experience inner split about the new thought. I call this *phony positivity*. In the case above an example of phony positivity might be:

"At first I thought he was funny-looking, but I bet if you look closer, he actually has lovely features." This could be a nice shift if it's actually true, but if it's just an attempt to smooth over a negative thought, it won't resonate. It's healthier to keep things real, even within our own minds.

When it comes to assessing (read: judging) others, unproductive negativity is often triggered by sensitive aspects of ourselves. For example, because I've always been self-conscious about my own tendency toward arrogance and superiority, I have a particular radar for and aversion to that quality in other people. On the other hand, I have a dear friend who is a truly modest soul, and she doesn't seem to notice or mind the posturing of others. It's not always our own vices that precipitate sensitivity; it could also be overexposure or yearning. I have a client who feels her mom has a fake sweetness about her. She will gush at people, but then mock them afterwards behind their backs. My client doesn't do this at all, but because of her mother's habit, she doesn't trust anything that feels like over-sweetness or phoniness in others and is probably more suspicious of it than the average person.

I am writing these words in 2017, following the historic presidential election of Donald J. Trump. This has been the most emotionally charged election that I can remember, perhaps of all time. Americans everywhere have weighed in on politics with an excitement rivaling feelings about reality television. This is not the time or place for an analysis of the ever-widening gap between the political right and left. But a major problem in terms of the current divisiveness of our country is that so many people have difficulty seeing the perspective of the other side. I decided to challenge myself to describe the political approaches of each in a way so even-handed that my reader would not be able to discern my political party. (I did not address the individual candidates, just the general political platforms of the parties.)

Left: Historical oppression of minority groups, poverty, inequality, abuse of power, and cruelty have generated social problems throughout history. While the gradual liberalization of the Western world has helped liberate women, people of color, LGBTQ individuals, immigrants, refugees, and other minorities from much discrimination and offered them many new opportunities, we still have a long way to go. An empowered government has the ability to help. We can enact legislation to promote more equality and opportunity, decrease military activity in favor of negotiation, embrace cultural diversity, and protect the natural environment. Women should have autonomy over their bodies, and easy, affordable access to abortion resources. We should open our doors to those less fortunate, and respect, help, and learn from them. We need to cultivate friendship and trust with the growing Islamic population, domestically and internationally, as a road to peace and unity. Radical change will improve our country.

Right: Our country is imperfect, but is a bastion of security, founded on a bedrock of vision, faith, freedom, and opportunity. Minority groups of all kinds have more rights, safety, and freedom here than virtually anywhere else on Earth. The smaller the government, the more meaningful individual liberty becomes. It is preferable not to kill unborn babies. The federal government's job should be limited, and should focus on providing physical safety, enabling free trade and economic prosperity, maintaining basic infrastructure and cooperation between state governments, protecting its citizens from outside danger, helping to spread the values of human rights across the globe, and supporting our allies overseas. While we should continue to engage in peace talks and negotiations, we also need to maintain a strong militia and solid borders to protect our citizens and legal immigrants from global terror, illegal labor, and drugs, violence, weapons, and other dangers.

How was that? Could you tell which way I voted? Did either description elicit strong feelings in you?

I want to point out that Horizon-shifting our thoughts about others can take different forms. Sometimes it's about giving the benefit of the doubt. At other times, it's about empathy. And still others, it's simply about acceptance.

It Wasn't About Me

I was walking through Costco a few years ago (writing this book has highlighted for me how much time I actually spend in Costco), and I passed by a woman I knew from college. We had been friendly back then, but she moved to an elegant part of town and became kind of fancy, and our paths didn't cross much after that. As we passed one another, I smiled at her and said hi, and she looked right past me. In my head was an instantaneous judgment: "Ok, I guess I'm just not cool enough for you now." Internal eye-roll.

A few aisles later, we were walking toward each other again, but this time she looked right at me as if coming out of a trance and said, "Oh! Hi, Elisheva, I'm so glad to bump into you! I've been going through something with one of my kids, and I'm totally consumed with it; if you have a minute, do you think I could get your advice?" It was clear that she hadn't even registered that I was there the first time, she was so preoccupied with worry about her child. It was not about me at all, but I didn't realize that, because I'm me, and I only saw my own perspective of the interaction. We chatted for a few minutes about her concern, I gave her a couple of names of child therapists, and we wished each other well.

Gifting vs. Swapping

I used to have a pet peeve about smiling at or greeting others without reciprocity. I was once in the local supermarket, and there was a particularly grumpy cashier. As she handed me my change, I said, "Thank you, have a great day." She literally grunted in response. So I said, "And, I will too, thanks!" The guy behind me chuckled. But as I walked out of the store that day, something dawned on me. I had always thought I was trying to be this friendly, emotionally generous person, gracing the world with my smile and cheer. But the truth was—and I didn't realize it until then—I was really just offering a swap. A tit-for-tat feel- good moment, if you will. I will proffer my sunny "good morning" wishes to you, but you had better reward me with the same. Or else I get to be judge-y and superior about you. Or maybe feel slighted and insecure.

That day, I confronted my ulterior motives for kindness and committed to try and offer my greetings to others as an unconditional gift. If they want to respond in kind, so be it. And if not, then maybe they're not the "talk to strangers" type, or maybe they have no cheer left to share, or maybe it's none of my beeswax and I can just be nice for free and move on with my day. After that, I realized the low-grade anxiety I'd been ignoring beneath the surface when venturing into the social world related to tracking others' reactions to my overtures. It was liberating to just do my part and move on.

Here is an example of the four possible interpretations of the interaction with the cashier:

1. *Below* **the Horizon:** "Well, isn't she just a ray of sunshine? That was so rude..."

2. **Phony Positivity/ Overkill:** "She's probably a really amazing person who is carrying a profound load in her life. Also she's hard of hearing."

3.   *On* **the Horizon:** "Hm. I was trying to be pleasant, and she didn't reply in kind. That was uncomfortable for me."

4.   *Above* **the Horizon:** "I was trying to be friendly, but for whatever reason, she wasn't up for engaging with me. I hope she's ok. My job isn't to evoke specific reactions from others, it's to be true to my values. If I choose to reach out to others, I'll try to do so with no strings attached."

Several years ago, I ordered a CD set from a wonderful writer and couples therapist named Dan Wile. One idea he shared in the realm of relationships, which was very similar to the Horizon model, was that we tend to have three general styles of broaching difficult subjects with our loved ones:

1.   **Adversarial**: This is when we address our concerns in a combative way; we basically pick a fight.

2.   **Avoidant**: This is when we simply avoid dealing the issue directly, but it almost always inevitably comes out in other more subtle or passive aggressive ways.

3.   **Collaborative**: This is when we look at the problem as something that we, as a team, can try to solve together.

Here is a real-world, interpersonal example applying these three styles:

Jackie is one of three sisters. They are very close and often make plans to meet for lunch and shopping in the city together. One day, Jackie's friend Joy mentions that she bumped into Jackie's sisters coming out of a movie together the other day. Jackie's gut instinct reaction was to feel excluded, hurt, and betrayed to have not been invited to the movie, almost as if they went behind her back. Here are some options for how she could choose to handle her feelings with them.

1. **Adversarial**: Confront them angrily, in person, or by phone or text, saying, "I can't believe I had to hear from Joy that the two of you went behind my back. I really thought we were close. I guess I can't trust you. Who knows what else you're saying and doing when I'm not there?"

2. **Avoidant**: When Jackie's sister calls to ask her to help her out with a carpool, which she could and would normally do with pleasure, she answers coldly, "I don't think that's gonna work for me today; I have plans to get my nails done."

3. **Collaborative**: Jackie could give them the benefit of the doubt and let it go, assuming there was an innocuous reason. Or, if she prefers to address it, she could mention to one or both of her sisters that she heard they'd seen the movie, and say something like, "Oh, how was it? I'd have loved to have gone with you guys." This way she could peacefully feel out what happened; there may a reasonable explanation for why she wasn't

invited, such as her sisters thinking she had another commitment that day. Or they may have just wanted to spend a little time together on their own. If it was the latter, Jackie could either choose to accept that despite feeling disappointed or calmly share that she felt excluded.

There are endless examples and scenarios that illustrate how we can train our brains to reinterpret interactions with others from the basis of healthier thinking. When we get in the habit of gracing ourselves with gentle judgment, it becomes a new mental language, and more natural to apply to others as well. The first step is to notice when our internal narrator is in a negative state. Once we have that meta-cognition — that insight of noticing and analyzing our own thoughts — we grant ourselves the authority to edit and improve them, to reflect a healthier perspective and sentiment.

Shifting a thinking style from *below* to *above* the Horizon of Healthy Function can sometimes happen by actively switching mental gears. In this age of constant, varied forms of telecommunication, we have a lot of interaction around phones, texts, emails, and messaging technology. How we reach out and respond generates much opportunity to examine and improve communication styles. By learning to think, feel, and express ourselves more effectively, we manage our relationships with ourselves and others more kindly and efficiently.

It's a win-win to generate healthier thoughts about our relationships, because it makes both us and the other party feel more comfortable in the relationship. When I'm quick to take offense, I feel bad, and they feel guilty and become either avoidant, defensive, or uncomfortably apologetic. That creates distance, not closeness. When I pause to consider and try to understand the other's perspective, I feel less hurt, and they get the benefit of the doubt. Either they did nothing wrong and we may continue to enjoy a healthy connection, or they were at fault and we can discuss it openly and clearly. Once that happens, an explanation or apology will be more authentic.

Here is an example of how to move from *below* the Horizon of Healthy Function to *on* or *above* the Horizon in the context of communications. Say Hannah didn't return my call. Instead of immediately thinking (judging), "It's so rude that she didn't return my call," I can switch to, "I guess she hasn't had a chance to call me back," or "I wonder if she got my message," or even, "I wonder why she didn't return my call." This will help with questioning, as opposed to accusing. So instead of saying to Hannah, "Don't you know it's rude to ignore people when they leave you a voicemail?!" I could say, "Hi, I don't know if you got my message, but here's what I wanted to ask you..."

When we need something from someone else, if we soften our demands into requests, our communication and relating will improve immensely. So, instead of, "I need you to call me back, ASAP!" we could substitute it with, "Could you please call me when you get a second? It's time sensitive—thanks!"

Another example: Last summer, I had a tough decision to make. The son of a close friend of mine, Mimi, was getting married. (Hi, Mim!) I don't have much to do with him, but in our community, showing up for parents of the bride and groom is expected even for second-tier friends, and this is a very close friend who's really been there for me over the years. The problem was, my brother and sister-in-law and their family were in from overseas and this was the only possible night for us to have a family gathering, the type that only happens once every few years. I wanted to be there for both, and even tried to coordinate the timing, but I saw it wasn't happening, as they were two hours away from each other. I really vacillated, but ultimately made the decision to be with my family, even though I felt awful for missing the wedding.

My friend was understandably disappointed. But when I called her afterwards, she could have had one of three types of reactions:

1. *Below* **the Horizon** (choosing to be offended and to remain in this position): "I can't believe you blew this off. How often does my son get married? After all we've been through and everything I've done for you... What a rotten thing to do! I'm really mad at you."

2. ***On*** **the Horizon** (simply acknowledging the reality and her feelings about it): "I was so surprised you didn't come; I was really looking forward to having you there and so disappointed that you weren't. I guess it is what it is."

3. ***Above*** **the Horizon** (expressing her feelings about it, but choosing to accept, understand, and move forward): "It was a real bummer not to have you there. It was such a special night, and I wanted you to be a part of it. But I get it—family comes first, and this was a rare opportunity. I know you would have wanted to be there. And while I'd have really loved to have you, we still had a great crowd of friends and family that came out to celebrate. The couple looks so happy, and I'm really grateful everything went so well. Next time we have a wedding I know you'll be there, and in the meantime, I can't wait to show you the pictures."

Fortunately for both of us, she chose Door #3.

Action vs. Acceptance in Supporting Others

I have a very wise friend named Chaya. We're both busy ladies, but sometimes we need a quick "phone session" with one another to talk something out. When one of us wants to hash out something specific, we call it, "taking the couch." One fine day, I called her and said,

"Can I have the couch for a few minutes?" She replied, "Sure, but before you start—is this something you want me to try to help you brainstorm advice about, or would you just like me to be here for you and listen?"

I thought that was such a brilliant question and have quoted her many times since then. That question forced me to focus on what I needed from that dialogue. Rather than just a vent or rant, I had to ask myself: What am I looking for right now? Do I want to go into problem-solving mode, or do I just need to talk out how I feel and have someone empathize and validate? (Or even challenge me? Chaya is that good a friend.) Once I determine what I feel I need in that moment, I can convey it to her, and then she can offer the right kind of support without wasting energy and time.

Some people prefer troubleshooting, while others prefer philosophizing, but most of us end up needing to do some of each. When we jump in to fix it, but our friend just wants a shoulder to cry on, we both end up feeling dissatisfied by the conversation. And conversely, when we nod and agree sympathetically, but the friend was looking for input or advice, we're also both left feeling unsettled. We can't read minds. Not only can't we read our friends' minds, but often we aren't even that aware of our own feelings or needs. So pausing to ask, "What do I or what does the other hope to gain from this interaction," can help clarify for more effective dialogue. In most cases, even when troubleshooting, a certain amount of listening, understanding, and validation will still be welcome, even just for the sake of being able to define and address the issue most practically.

On Being a Work in Progress

When I look back at my own writing through the years, I notice an interesting, and at first counter-intuitive, pattern: The further back I go, the more preachy and dogmatic my writing is—to the point where I cringe a little (or sometimes a lot). Looking back and rereading words I penned and opined as a young adult, they now feel over-confident, bossy and pretentious. Worse, I don't even necessarily agree with all of my younger self's assertions anymore! So much so, that it gives me pause speaking and writing now; how will I feel about these words when I'm seventy- five?

One might have guessed the opposite — that the writing of a new professional would be humble and unassuming, but as she gains knowledge, experience, and success, the confidence emerges in her material. That may be true for some people. But I've found for myself and for others that the more I learn, the less sure I am of things, and the more open I am to being proven wrong, and the more space I can hold for dissenting opinion. That can be scary when trying to establish a position on anything. It was liberating to discover that for most of us, beliefs are dynamic, not static; they are organic and continuously evolving, not carved in stone. And so I've been learning to (try to) suggest, rather than prescribe, and to do so in a softer, more open-minded way.

Learning from the Kids

It helps that like most others, my kids tend to age chronologically. A young child needs more direct instruction and guidance than a teenager. And so while my children were younger, I was in the habit of determining and letting them know what they needed to do, but as they got older, I wanted to give over more and more freedom and autonomy while still being a resource for them.

For example: Let's say my five-year-old son wants to invite a friend over. He calls the friend and there's no answer. He wants to keep calling every five minutes to see if they're home yet. It's my job as the mom to explain why his friend's family might not appreciate their phone ringing off the hook for a five-year-old playdate. He may or may not accept my logic, but I feel it is my job to protect both his friend and him from the socially inappropriate behavior of incessant calling. When it comes to a preschooler in that sort of situation, mom calls the shots. (In my house, I mean. You are welcome to allow your tots to harass their friends as long as they're not friends with my kids.)

My 15-year-old, on the other hand, mentions to me that he's gone running with a certain friend a couple of times last week. He enjoyed it and would like to go again, but he noticed that the last few times he got together with this guy, he was the one who initiated making the plans. He wants to know if I think he should wait for the other guy to call this time, just to be sure it's really a two-way interest in the friendship. As a Jewish mother, I have a strong temptation to take the wheel when it comes to my kids' lives. (And every else's. Wait—was that a micro-aggression against myself?) And if he's offering it to me, how can I resist?

But I try hard to remember in these moments, that as much as I would love to raise kids who do what I believe is right, the reality is that ultimately, I want to raise kids who will do what *they* believe is right (and I really hope we agree). So rather than immediately telling him, "I think you should hold off and call another friend," or "Why don't you just send a casual text inviting him for a weekly run?" I aim to reflect his deliberation and validate both options.

From Auto-thoughts, to Meta-thoughts, to Replacement Thoughts

Expressing ourselves to others in a healthy, collaborative, productive, and authentic way begins with calibrating how we formulate thoughts in our own minds.

The initial thought that pops into our heads without any invitation is what I think of as an "auto-thought"—a spontaneously and naturally occurring thought. Most of the time, these auto-thoughts are either helpful or harmless, and they either play out naturally or fizzle on their own. For example, "I'm kind of thirsty," might lead to me to take a glass of water, and then the thought has served its purpose and moves along. Another auto-thought, "I'd love to go to the beach today!" might be followed by, "but it's February in New York, it's freezing, it's Wednesday, and I have to work, dang it." And that thought puffs into irrelevant oblivion.

Sometimes, we have a thought about our auto-thought, which we could call a "meta-thought." An example of an auto- thought/meta-thought shift would be the following.

1. **Auto-thought:** "I can't believe I made that mistake! I'm so stupid!"

2. **Meta-thought**: "I shouldn't be calling myself stupid, even if my own head—I know negative self-talk isn't good for me."

3. **Replacement (corrected) thought:** "So, I goofed. That was a silly mistake. But now I'll try to fix it and learn from it for next time."

A good way to know when we're thinking *below* the Healthy Horizon is when we find ourselves using extreme or generalizing language:

- "He always does this!"
- "She never does that!"
- "That's the worst thing that could have happened!"
- "I feel like I'm gonna die!"

When we catch our brains doing that, we can meta-think to correct and then calibrate with more moderate, accurate, and healthy language. For each of the above four examples, we could substitute something like the following (respectively):

- "It feels like this happens often."
- "I don't remember her doing that much."
- "This is not what I would have wanted."
- "I'm feeling drained and discouraged."

These techniques are applicable in a variety of scenarios.

Catastrophizing and Trivializing

In general, the human mind has two opposing tendencies when conceptualizing things: catastrophizing and trivializing.

Catastrophizing:

Sometimes, our disappointments, frustrations, fears, or resentments can loom larger than life in our minds. This could take the form of exaggerated representation of the actual situation or an inflated emotional response. The danger of catastrophizing events and incidents, of course, is the risk of wasting precious time and energy on unworthy stressors.

My own tendency to catastrophize usually revolves around my kids. I wrote this section on a laptop in a pavilion overlooking Goblin Valley, a fascinatingly bizarre rock formation in the magnificent Utah mountains, on our summer trip. My husband and children were hiking the trail with some family friends. Often when we set off on a hike, I need to consciously attend to my brain's tendency to imagine the worst, most dangerous and tragic possible scenarios that could occur. When someone's sneaker slips on a rock or trips on a branch, my heart skips a beat. I am catastrophizing the potential hazards of a reasonably safe activity. Because I know that I tend to do this in these situations, I try to respond to my brain's dramatic tendencies with logic. This is a worrying, or anxious, form of catastrophizing. That is my particular brain's favorite type.

While I was sitting and writing at this beautiful site, trying to think of another good example of mental catastrophizing, a large family of tourists arrived for a picnic, arranging themselves noisily around the other tables and loudly bantering in a foreign language. I had been enjoying the quiet solitude, the sacred communion with nature (and my laptop…), and this was an unwelcome intrusion. (Because apparently, I own this lookout spot.) My brain immediately got annoyed, micro-catastrophizing with thoughts like, "Oh no! I had a rare, precious two hours in which to write uninterrupted, and now this distraction is going to rob me of my flow and concentration. What a wasted opportunity! Don't these people have somewhere else they could be that wouldn't be sabotaging my work??" Turns out they were actually supplementing it- I should thank them for this paragraph.

Catastrophizing is when we take something unpleasant and, in our minds, make it bigger and more upsetting than it needs to be, thereby adding unnecessary stress to our situation.

Trivializing:

At the other end of the distortion spectrum is trivializing. This is when we minimize a problem to make it less than it is. Sometimes trivializing can be helpful. When there is a minor inconvenience, and our first instinct is to get unduly aggravated, minimizing self- talk can help us move past it more quickly. But sometimes trivializing means invalidated our own legitimate feelings.

For example, one of my clients, Maurice, was let go from the company where he'd been working for thirteen years. He didn't see it coming and wasn't sure what he would be able to do next. When I asked him if he was ok, he replied, "Sure, I'm fine. I can't complain. People have much more serious problems than this. It's not a big deal— I guess I'll just have to look for a new job." That sounds really good-natured and true, and on the surface it is. The problem was, he then picked up smoking again and didn't return calls from his girlfriend for the next two weeks. Because he was trivializing the impact of losing his job, he wasn't dealing with his deeper feelings, and they were coming out in other areas of his life.

If Maurice had catastrophized his situation, instead of trivializing it, it may have sounded like this: "I just wasted the past thirteen years of my life barking up the wrong tree. I thought I would be able to advance and grow old working in that company, and they just cut me loose, threw me out like an expired yogurt. I don't know what I'll do; I'll probably lose my car, my home, and will end up penniless on the street. My life is over…"

What I try to remind my clients, my children, and myself is this:

Don't make it bigger than it is, don't make it smaller than it is; take it for what it is, and then figure out what to do with it.

This practice is so important, it's worth repeating:

Don't make it bigger than it is, don't make it smaller than it is; take it for what it is, and then figure out what to do with it.

My daughter, Nava, is a delightful young lady with a passionate nature. (I am, of course, totally objective and unbiased.) She feels the highs and lows of life experience with an intensity she inherited from her mom. Sometimes she feels sad or disappointed about something not turning out the way she would have liked— say, hypothetically, a parent siding with her little sister in an argument. Most of the time, she is resilient and easy-going, but sometimes she'll take herself off to the side of her room, her sweet little face will crinkle up, and she'll give way to sorrowful tears. We call it, "feeling tragic."

A great thing about Nava is her ability to have perspective. When she gets like this over a minor trigger, I can say to her, "Nava, are you feeling tragic?" At that point she will smile through her tears and crumpled cheeks, crook her head a little to one side, and nod knowingly. She understands that her feelings don't define her reality. She can feel with all the depth of her 11-year-old heart and still have the maturity to understand that this is just a moment, it will pass, and she'll be ok. She has learned not to take her dramatic feelings too seriously. She knows she can certainly feel them, but also understands that allowing herself to be overtaken by them will not serve her well. This perspective allows her to indulge in a good cry, express her tragic feelings and interpretations about how a particular sister may have a tendency to "ruin her whole life," and then hug it out and move on.

Another daughter, Sussy, has a different tendency. She is so peace-loving, even within herself, that she often too quickly tries to make everything ok. When the kids are bickering about who has to sit in the back row of the minivan, she's usually the first to volunteer; not because she likes it, but because she likes peace.

I remember when she was about two-and-a-half years old, she very much wanted to get her ears pierced. We told her that it would hurt, but she really wanted those earrings. So we took her to the pediatrician's office and had them pierce her ears. Brave little Sussy held my hand, flinched a bit, and took it like a pro. Afterwards, I asked her if she was ok. She forced her sweet little face into an unconvincing smile and replied, "Yeah! It barely hurt at all! And they're so pretty." I saw her hands gingerly reaching up to soothe her sore little earlobes. Later in the day, she came to me again and said, "Mommy? I love my new earrings, but they actually do hurt a little." Then I held her, she had a little cry, and we moved on. Her tendency is to trivialize, to make mountains into molehills, to quickly forgive and forget. It makes her a pleasure to be around, but she sometimes needs to remember to acknowledge her feelings so they don't wear her down.

Serenity Now, Please: A Story About Traffic

A few months ago, I was scheduled to give a lecture in Manhattan, which is about an hour from my home. I do this drive fairly frequently, since my parents live there. As a card-carrying time-worrier, I left at 6:07 p.m. for an 8:00 p.m. talk. I was particularly jittery about this talk because it was in the community where I grew up; my mom and a lot of her friends were going to be there. And it was about sex, so- y'know, a nice easy topic. About seven minutes into the drive, I passed our local Costco. (There it is again!) At least, I tried to pass our local Costco, but the cars were at a complete standstill. I was in the middle of three lanes jam-packed with brake lights. Even the honking petered out after a while.

At first, I got antsy. Then I got nervous. After forty-five minutes and not even passing the "t" in the Costco sign, I started to feel panicky. I had done things right: I had left myself plenty of time, taken the most direct route, even used a navigation app that usually takes traffic patterns into consideration. I thought of calling the host to explain my delay and offering to Skype in from the car if necessary. At a certain point, I realized astutely that for some reason, my rising stress level was doing literally zero to move the other cars along. I realized that one of two things was going to happen: I would make it to the lecture, or I would not make it to the lecture. In either case, no one would die, most probably. The outcome was completely outside of my locus of control.

I happen to be a person of faith, and so my particular version of Horizon-shifting often includes some variation of "Let go and let God," but if you don't happen to believe in God, it works well with "the universe," "life," or "nature," too. Once we can acknowledge our limitations, embrace that humility, and ease into working with what we CAN do, we can conserve energy and better focus.

Remember the famous Serenity Prayer from the 12-Step program for addiction treatment: "God grant me the serenity to accept the things I cannot change; courage to change the things I can; and wisdom to know the difference"? While this has not helped me much with my Hershey's addiction, it is the perfect antidote to moments like that drive to the city. I couldn't control the traffic on the road, but I could decide whether I wanted to panic about it. The moment that thought occurred to me, I could feel the change in my mind and body. I immediately relaxed and decided to be ok with whatever the outcome.

I've had more profound moments of surrender than that, but I chose this one specifically because it was a relatively low-risk situation; no one would get hurt if I missed my lecture, and it would have just been an inconvenience and a financial loss. But in that moment, the urgency overtook me, and my adrenaline responded in kind. Once I reminded myself that nothing serious was at stake, and more importantly, there was nothing I could do, I was able to relax into the uncertainty of waiting for the traffic to clear, to find out whether I would get there in time. (I arrived at 8:01 p.m. and it went well, thanks.)

An Unlikely Lesson from My Chemistry Teacher

As a sophomore in high school, I remember exactly where I was standing with some friends in the dingy hallway of our school: right next to the pay phone near the main office. We were examining our elective request forms and comparing the pros and cons regarding which classes to take. I complained to my friends, "It's such a shame—the classes I want to take are up against one another in time slots, so I won't be able to take all the classes that I want." At that moment, my chemistry teacher happened to be passing by and overheard my comment. She stopped and looked at me. "Elisheva, what a wonderful problem!" she exclaimed in her distinctively high-pitched voice, and then walked away. At the time, I was puzzled, thinking, "No, it's actually annoying that I can't take all the classes that I want."

Over time, I came to understand what she meant by that. Most of us are in a constant state of managing the level of stimulation in our lives, either seeking out more or scaling back to maintain a certain equilibrium. Some people struggle with understimulation, or boredom. There isn't much that interests them or that they feel pulled to do. Others struggle with overstimulation, feeling pulled by too many interests or possibilities. The risk of understimulation in its extreme form is laziness or depression; the risk of chronic overstimulation is anxiety or burnout.

That day with the electives sheet was an example of a theme in my life. There are usually too many things I want to do. In its healthiest form, I become inspired, ambitious, creative, and industrious. When I drop *below* my Horizon, I get fragmented, frazzled, frustrated, and overwhelmed. I have friends and colleagues who are wired the same way; there is just always so much we want to do at any given time.

The flipside of this quality is understimulation, which might include a sense of ennui or restlessness. My friend, who is wired this way, is a more laid-back, relaxed, contented soul. She is happy to sit on her porch, watching the branches sway in the wind. Other times, she struggles with feeling down, unfocused, and wanting to sleep too much. Even basic responsibilities or recreational opportunities seem like a burden to her. She sometimes struggles with a sense of purposelessness, not really knowing what to do with herself.

In a sense, these are just different moods of the same personality traits, but moods can be manipulated by thoughts. Moods are essentially feelings that decided to stick around for a while. And feelings are almost always generated by thoughts. Even when our moods and feelings are precipitated by external events, or interactions with others, ultimately it's our thoughts about them that generate ensuing feelings and moods. A consistent pattern of moods is what comprises our general demeanor. A combination of nature and nurture will determine what sort of general temperament we begin with, but the way we direct, delve into, or dismiss our thoughts and feelings forges our personalities.

As children, we tend to think much the way we breathe: automatically and without much concentration. The vast majority of our thoughts are "auto-thoughts"— thoughts that pop into our heads either spontaneously or in response to a stimulus. Those thoughts will either move along or morph into deeper, related thoughts and feelings, and then occasionally moods. Most kids don't give a lot of meta-thought to their internal, cognitive lives.

Once we're older, we tend to reflect more consciously about our thoughts and feelings, either because we are taught to do so, or because we mature into this self-awareness. By acknowledging the thoughts that create the feelings that affect us, we begin to gain access to self-authorship. But what do we do about the narratives from our childhoods?

CHAPTER 4:

Mental Memoirs and Moving Forward

You know how people often say: "Live in the moment! There's no time like the present"? I definitely hear their point, but at the same time, today's moment was the result of lots of previous moments and will determine the outcome of lots of future moments. I've considered ordering a bumper sticker for my car, saying: "I strive to live each day as if it's my last. That's why I never fold the laundry." For years I've been thinking that there's got to be a balance between being all fragmented about the past and the future, but also only living for today.

Narrative therapy is based on the idea that each of us is living out a unique and subjective story. The events that happen outside our bodies are processed and stored in our memories and inform the way we relate to our past, present, and future realities.

I sometimes tell clients that one definition of anxiety is: "Allowing either the past or the future to smoosh out the present." (Smoosh is a real word- google it.) Regretting, resenting, reliving, and re- experiencing the past in unhelpful ways can take us away from who we are trying to be today. Living in the past can poison us. On the flipside, worries, fears, and obsessive planning about the future also deprives us of being present in the here and now. Past and future have their places, and we need to learn and plan, but we are always only living *now.*

Of course, we can't all sit on a mountaintop meditating to achieve Zen mindfulness all the time. That would get squishy. We sometimes need to relate to the past or consider the future; these are important aspects of our narratives. In this chapter, we will look at both problematic and healthier ways of narrating the tenses and learn how to edit the narrative to bring it *above* the Horizon.

Our *mental memoirs* are the stories that our thoughts and feelings write in our own minds and hearts about our pasts. They get automatically edited and amended by the mechanics of memory and forgetting, along with the red pen of hindsight.

Sometimes these omissions and generalizations are helpful to us. There are cases of individuals who have excruciatingly precise autobiographical memories. It can actually be psychologically exhausting to carry around our mental memoirs in living color with the detail, feeling, and accuracy that we had as we lived them. They say women often clean up the memories of childbirth, because we'd rather remember the day our progeny arrive with joy than with agony. We sometimes remember happy times through rose-colored lenses or sanitize awful experiences to minimize the pain of recall. Some things are better off forgotten or vaguely catalogued in the deep recesses of our sub- or preconscious memories.

But there are times when our cognitive distortions impact the way we remember and narrate our own personal histories in ways that can inhibit healthy living. We each enter into a story in progress at birth. Whether in a biological or adoptive family, we become the next chapter in the narratives of others, and for the first number of years, much of our reality is designed and determined by those powerful "others." For many of us, our families did the best they could to provide a safe, healthy, caring, loving environment for us. For others, the attempt was made but perhaps not successful. Still others were raised, neglected, or abused in toxic home environments. And others may have been raised in loving homes, but encountered trauma from other sources. One thing is for sure: We all meet up with adversity at some point or another. It would be wonderful if all this pain and suffering would vanish, but as long as utopia is not our reality, we need to learn how to cope.

My oldest son, Shmuel, loves to study history, and it's something I admire. I once mentioned to him that I value the idea of understanding the global past. But that I've made efforts to study it, yet the facts just don't stick in my brain, so I don't end up knowing history well. Without missing a beat, he replied: "Well, then you may be doomed to repeat it," in his trademark, deadpan wit.

Our pasts are incredibly important parts of our narratives, not only because they are formative in how we develop, but also because we tend to use them to view and shape the future. While we can't change what happened to us or what we've already done, we can decide to revisit how we want to relate to it all, and what we want to do presently and going forward. As they say, "Those who don't study history are doomed to repeat it." And, "we are what our parents make us," but it's our own choice whether to stay that way.

Whether we have charmed childhoods, minor setbacks, larger challenges, or full-on trauma or tragedy, here are several ways we tend to distort these into our life narratives:

1. **<u>Victimhood</u>**: Whether fully justified or absurdly dramatized, it can sometimes feel oddly good to identify as a victim in the short term. Victimhood holds others accountable for our pain and excuses our own role in later troubling or painful events. The problem with long-term victimhood is that pity parties tend to leave nasty hangovers and can hold us back from empowered living. When we go into victim mindset, we wallow, get blamey, and often shirk responsibility for moving beyond the "stuff." So when I find myself indulging in too much victim-flavored thinking, I try to call myself out on it, regroup, and rescript.

2. **<u>Denial, forgetting, or repression:</u>** While there are differences between these, technically, they all

involve a rejection of reality. This, too, can be helpful and adaptive in the short term, but can often come back to bite us eventually. When we don't even realize that we're repressing something from the past, it can sometimes manifest in unpleasant symptoms, physical malaise, or general emotional disturbance. In that case, it might take some psychological excavation or detective work to find and treat the cause.

3. **<u>Trivializing</u>**: This is when we try to make the stories of our past "smaller" than they were, less significant and less meaningful, to minimize their impact and shrink their import. This can happen with the good, the bad, or the ugly. It can appear as a healthy adaptation in the form of humility, stoicism, or courage. But when we trivialize reality, we're being internally dishonest, and then we often pay a price. To say "it wasn't that bad," if it in fact was, is to call into question one's sense of agency and personal experience. If we want to process, grow from, and transcend life's obstacles, we need to first view them honestly.

4. **<u>Exaggerating</u>**: This is the opposite of trivializing. It's making history larger than life, attributing catastrophic, grandiose, or distorted qualities to the memories and their repercussions. These reverberations don't serve us well, again, because a dishonest rendering of our experiences deprives us of the ability to properly integrate them.

5. **<u>Self-blaming:</u>** This, in a way, is the opposite of self- victimizing. It's assuming blame, fault, guilt, shame, and responsibility for stories beyond the scope of our control.

6. **<u>Obsessing</u>**: While the varying forms of OCD deserve and, in fact, have books of their own, the tendency to overfocus on a specific episode or theme from the past is not limited to the clinically obsessional. Obsessing is when a thought, idea, or memory is taking up more mental real estate than it deserves.

7. **<u>Selective memory:</u>** None of us has a perfectly accurate memory; we all draft our mental memoirs in spliced vignettes. But selective memory can be a problem when the scenes, interactions, thoughts, feelings, and anecdotes that we remember are skewed along a particular theme or agenda, again, for better or for worse.

Having listed and defined these cognitive tendencies, let's look at some narrative examples, or *mental memoirs,* of each of them in action. (Warning: please forgive the nerdy name alliteration.)

Case Study 1: Valerie the Victim

Valerie is the middle of three sisters, close in age. Their parents were busy professionals, and the girls constantly vied for attention and approval. Valerie remembers her childhood years sadly:

"Sabrina was the smart one. My big sister was always setting the gold standard with straight A's. It was so hard to follow in her footsteps. Melinda was a little princess, the pretty, lovely one. They indulged her with awesome clothes, which only made her more vain. I was a B student and only 'average' pretty. I was always lost in the shuffle. Sabrina was boasted about in the bumper stickers, Mel got all the visual attention, and I never felt like I had much to show for myself. No one saw any good in me.

"I know my parents loved and cared about me, and they were probably even proud of me, but I am really nothing special. I get along OK with my sisters, and I had plenty of friends. But I always felt so plain and ordinary. I guess that's why I never bother to try. I dropped out of college, and I never pursued a career, because it would never be as impressive as Sabrina's. I don't invest much in my personal presentation because even if I really make an effort, like, get a great haircut, buy cute clothes and accessories, exercise and eat right, I just end up comparing myself to gorgeous Mel and feeling frumpy and awkward. So I just coast along, being invisible and unimpressive."

Valerie revisited:

Valerie the Victim used her stellar sisters to justify her lackluster approach to life and trying. The three formulations of her narrative could be summarized as follows:

1. *Below* **the Horizon:** "My sisters are naturally gifted and celebrated, and I'm dull and unimportant. Since I don't have the advantages that they do, I will never amount to anything or feel good about myself, so there's no point in trying."

Pretty depressing, right? Let's see if she can reach that lifeboat.

2. *On* **the Horizon:** "Growing up, I didn't feel great about myself, especially sandwiched between sisters who were each able to shine. I didn't feel valuable, and I find that it affects my self-esteem and sense of ambition even today."

See how we removed the whiny violins in the second take? Next is an even healthier version.

3. *Above* **the Horizon:** "Over the years, I often felt inferior to my sisters. I see how I tend to get down on myself about not feeling special even now as an adult. Sometimes I really let it get me down. I guess my challenge is to figure out who I am or want to be. I may not be naturally brilliant or beautiful, but that doesn't make me useless. I'd like to see if I can find something I can be good at, enjoy, or feel good about, and see how I

can define myself without constantly grading or comparing myself to them."

The third version incorporates an acknowledgement of the problem, but adds the element of self-determination through "I" statements, which express choice, hope, and productive vision for change.

One last version will illustrate "aiming" too high—the overly- sunny, Pollyanna-style approach:

"Sabrina and Melinda each have always had their areas of strength, but I know in my heart that I'm extraordinary in my own way, and it's what's inside that counts. Really I'm a hidden rock star." There is nothing inherently wrong with this sentence. But after seeing the *below* the Horizon starting point, a statement like this one feels inauthentic to her experience—it invalidates her struggle and whitewashes the process of redefining her sense of self.

Case Study 2: Debbie the Denier

Debbie is a smiley, friendly, accommodating, nervous young woman. She is a dedicated office manager in a busy law practice. She grew up in a toxic home environment, seeing her mother verbally and sometimes physically abused by her father. She never really shared much about this with her boyfriend, Dillan, because she didn't think it was anything out of the ordinary. Even when her brother moved out of the house angrily at sixteen, yelling about how he wanted to get as far away from their dad as possible, Debbie just chalked it up to his "teenage hormonal rebellion." Debbie loves her parents and describes them as "traditional."

Dillan thinks Debbie is terrific and very compatible with him because they really seem to think so similarly. But after a few months, he worries if it's too good to be true. He notices that she *never* disagrees with him. When he expresses disagreement with her, she usually changes her mind to match his. And sometimes when he tries to touch her unexpectedly, she jumps back. If he ever gets even a little upset about anything, she somehow "gets busy" and unavailable for a few days, ignoring his calls or texts.

When Dillan came to Debbie's family for Thanksgiving dinner, he witnessed clearly how unkindly her father treated her mother and how broken her mom seemed. After they left, he tried to mention it to her in the car, and Debbie's reply was, "Oh, you just don't understand the older generation. They're really happy together; they just have their own way of showing their love." Dillan suggested that maybe Debbie was overly agreeable because she felt she had to be, having grown up seeing her mom always cowed by her dad. Debbie thought for a moment, and then replied, "Maybe—I don't know, though. They're happy, we're happy, it's all good in the end." When he later tried to visit the issue again, Debbie disappeared with a "stomach bug" for four days.

Debbie Revisited:

Debbie is in denial about the power imbalance she witnessed in her parents' marriage growing up. She continues to deny the problem, perhaps because there isn't much she can do about it anyway. Generally, letting go of a problem that we can't solve is a healthy move. But when it's so close to home, not even acknowledging that it's there, or the effect that it has had on Debbie, seems to be inhibiting her ability to be honest in her relationships with Dillan. Her go-to narrative is the overly-sunny one: "They're just traditional; it works for them, so it's all good." But she avoids conflict at all costs, and when she bumps up against any potential conflict, she becomes avoidant.

1. *Below* **the Horizon:** "My dad dominates my mom because he's a bully, and my mom's a wimp. I guess the only way to be safe in a relationship is to make sure to never challenge your man. Or maybe relationships are not worth the risk."

The unhealthy lesson she learns from her parents is to be subservient or avoidant.

2. *On* **the Horizon:** "My parents have the kind of marriage that makes me nervous to trust. Even though Dillan is not my dad, I usually just slip into over-accommodating mode, just to keep the peace."

In this case she has the perspective that not all relationships follow her parents' template, but she still recognizes how parts of her personality evolved along that paradigm.

3.   *Above* **the Horizon:** "Dillan noticed that I don't seem to stand my ground very much. I never realized how much my mom's style of being in a relationship sort of rubbed off on me. I guess seeing my parents' slanted marriage got me in the mindset and habit of just trying to keep the peace. It's just second nature to me, but Dillan might have a point—it might be healthier for me to challenge myself to be more honest, to figure out how I feel about things, to take the chance of expressing a differing opinion and it being ok to disagree. I love my parents, and there is much I can learn from each of them as people, but now that I revisit this as an adult, I don't think their relationship is the best model for me."

In the healthy construct, Debbie sees the impact of her parents on her relational style, but is now willing to try and create a more empowered approach for herself.

Case Study 3: Troy the Trivializer

Troy is a 24-year-old CPA in a mid-level Manhattan accounting firm. From the age of ten, he was raised in a loving home, sent to good schools, and had nice friends.

Before he was ten, though, he was bounced around the foster care system. Taken from his unemployed, addicted single mom at the age of four, he remembers little about his life with her, though he's had a few supervised visits with her. He mostly remembers being scared. The foster families varied from well-meaning, to apathetic, to downright cruel. By a miracle, the last family that fostered him really began to love him and petitioned to adopt him. He was so happy and grateful that he was determined to try his best to make them proud. He told himself that whatever happened before he was ten didn't matter; now that he was safe and had opportunities, he was going to behave his best, work hard, and "deserve" his new life.

Throughout middle school and high school, Troy was a poster child for success. He never complained, and always played by the rules. During college, he developed some anxiety symptoms, and then he had a minor breakdown while studying for the CPA exam. When he was referred for counseling, the therapist asked him what it had been like for him as a young child, before the adoption. He sighed and responded:

"Sometimes it was OK. Sometimes not so OK. It wasn't easy, and I was scared a lot. But I know that I'm one of the lucky ones. I got adopted at ten by great people who really cared and gave me everything. That's more than enough. Whatever happened before, I know it was rough. But people have been through so much worse, without getting the lucky break that I did. So I made a decision to put that part of my past in a box and focus on the blessings. I don't see why it needs to have a place in my life now."

Troy Revisited:

Troy's noble decision to leave the past behind is coming from a place of strength and resilience. The concept is terrific. But to dismiss or minimize what he had been through as a child was to almost ignore or disqualify a formative part of his development. Let's look at his Horizon process and the three formulations:

1. *Below* **the Horizon:** "I have essentially led a life of great privilege. There are people out there with real problems and no way out. I got a 'get out of jail free card,' and I need to appreciate that and use it well. I have no right to let a few measly years from so long ago interfere with the opportunities I've been given. It doesn't matter what was, it only matters what is now."

This is a tricky one, because in theory it sounds empowering. But the truth is, Troy is negating something important and thereby not honoring a piece of the history that brought him to where he is today. And that seems to be taking a toll on him.

2. *On* **the Horizon:** "I know I had a rough beginning of life, and I remember that. I just would have hoped that all the love I got

afterwards, and all I've been able to accomplish as a result of that, could have healed me from that. But I see I carry some battle scars inside anyway."

Here, Troy is acknowledging that all is not entirely well—not in his past and not in his present. He is also relating to the gifts he's received, but he hasn't yet tried to integrate the two. Now let's head upward.

3.   *Above* **the Horizon:** "Ever since my adoption, I have felt an incredible sense of gratitude and opportunity. I've tried my utmost to lead the best life possible, to achieve good things, and to make my parents proud. I had always thought I could just start life from the age of ten onward. But I see that I'm carrying some pain, and it's affecting/impacting my well-being now. I'm also realizing that coming from a difficult early background has affected me. Maybe I appreciate the life I have now more because I've known a darker alternative. I think part of me is ashamed of those years. Either way, it might be time for me to acknowledge that little boy I used to be and invite him to join me in my good life now, instead of abandoning him to the place of memories I'd rather forget. I think that maybe once I can think and write about how that felt for me back then, I can really relax and enjoy what I have now. It will also help me to achieve from a

sense of personal fulfillment, rather than a sense of beholdenness and obligation."

Case Study: Evan the Exaggerator

Evan is at the table with his drinking buddies, playing cards half- heartedly while a football game hisses on the TV in the background. The guys are discussing sports and what they used to play. Evan adds, "I was quarterback for the varsity team in my high school back in the day. I was basically promised a free ride to an awesome college. The scouts were all over my talent, and I thought I might even have a shot at the NFL. Then one day, one game, I got taken down, busted up my knee so bad I needed three surgeries just to walk right again. The season was over for me, and I lost everything. I never got over that—I always think about what would have been. I could have been on that screen instead of here watching it."

A sad, plausible story, except that also seated at the table is Evan's classmate from high school. He remembers Evan warming the bench at school games and then twisting his ankle on prom night while attempting a showy dance move. He's pretty sure there were some crutches for a couple of weeks, and that prom was in May—well after football season. Evan was rewriting history, out of a desire to taste glory, even "thwarted" glory.

<u>Evan Revisited:</u>

Evan had tried to rewrite his own history as a "could have been."

Here are the three versions of his narrative.

1. ***Below* the Horizon:** "I could have had an illustrious career as a pro athlete. I was so amazing, but due to tragic bad luck, all that was ripped away; and poor me, here I am now, looking back at how great it could have been."

Isn't that depressing? Let's find an alternative.

2. ***On* the Horizon:** "Looking back on my high school years, I wonder if I could have applied myself to football more and maybe had a chance at a career in sports. I don't know if I really would have been able to get there, but it had been a dream, and I'm not sure I really gave myself the chance to try."

A little more realistic, right? Let's take it up a notch.

3. ***Above* the Horizon:** "When I watch football on TV, I remember playing for my high school varsity team and fantasizing about having a shot at becoming a pro. I don't know if I was really good enough, but sometimes it feels so real, I can almost taste it—the possibility, the excitement, and the disappointment of that not being a reality. I guess football really meant a lot to me

back then; I wonder if there's a way for me to play ball for pleasure and exercise these days, or to find another outlet that could give me that sort of workout and adrenaline rush."

I meet a lot of moms in particular who harbor wistful illusions of what they "might have been" if they'd gone to grad school or nurtured a career instead of their families. Sometimes these stories ring accurate, and other times they sound somewhat exaggerated. But in either case, sulking over what "could have been" rarely gets anyone anywhere. It's always better to relate practically to the reality that is, and try to achieve as much as possible within the parameters of the present and future.

Case Study: Sophia the Self-Blamer

Sophia remembers hearing her parents arguing loudly from the time she was a little girl. Although they usually closed the door to their bedroom, she could often make out phrases and snippets of their fights, and she always perked up and then cringed when she heard her own name. She felt terrible because ever since the school counselor had diagnosed her with dyslexia, she knew her parents were spending extra money that they couldn't really afford on private tutors and that they didn't agree on how to manage it.

When her mother finally left her father, it emerged that she had been secretly developing a romantic relationship with another dad in the neighborhood. She'd technically met this man through Sophia because his daughter was on her soccer team. While she doesn't say it out loud, Sophia has always felt that she was the reason her parents' marriage fell apart. It was, after all, a result of her dyslexia, her expenses, her soccer friend. After her mom left them, her dad became depressed, and Sophia felt it was up to her to make sure he got up for work, showered, ate dinner, turned off the TV, and went to bed. He had frequent headaches, so she kept the noise level low and lights dim, so as not to distress him.

Sophia has friends, but always worries about inconveniencing them. She also over-empathizes with their problems, which generates internal pressure, so she often keeps some emotional distance. She has become the sort of person who interjects the word "sorry" into conversations, the way most of us say "um." Every so often she wonders why she feels so guilty and emotionally exhausted, when all she has ever tried to do was go about her life and help people.

Sophia Revisited:

Here are Sophia's three narrative formulations:

1. *Below* **the Horizon**: "I carry a tremendous sense of guilt about what a burden I was on my parents. I was basically the reason my family came apart. If I only could have figured out how

to read like everyone else, or not been so self-absorbed that I needed to play soccer, my mom and dad might still be together and happily married."

As people removed from this story, it's easy for us to see how inaccurate Sophia's perceptions are. But when we look in our own mental mirrors, some of us might find that we tend to blame ourselves for existing or for other people's problems. Here is a softer version:

2.   ***On* the Horizon:** "I know it's not my fault, yet I can't help but notice that a lot of what my parents fought about during their marriage centered around me and my needs. Even my mom's affair came about through an acquaintance of mine. I don't like the way that feels; I'm wondering if having me in their lives was too much of a strain on their marriage. And now I see a pattern in my own relationships of not ever wanting to impose."

In that one, Sophia acknowledges her feelings and tendencies, and doesn't take ownership for her parents' issues, but also doesn't take action to change her own response. Let's see if we can get it off the water.

3.   ***Above* the Horizon:** "Emotionally, I sometimes feel the weight of my parents' breakup as if it were resting on my own shoulders. In times like that, I need to remember that I was just a kid,

trying the best I could, and they were adults, making their own choices. It's sad that they couldn't save their marriage, and maybe parenting was too much for them, but in the end that was a choice they made. It's also sad that my dad kind of fell apart after that, but that wasn't something I caused. I need to remind myself that I can always only try my best. That the people in my life who care about me today want to be there for me, just like I want to be there for them. I will try to apologize only when I've actually done something wrong, and the rest of the time, allow myself to be, without shame or blame."

Nice work, Sophia.

Case Study: Oscar the Obsessor

Oscar has a good job with the local fire department, and enjoys a loving, committed relationship with his fiancée, Karen, who works next door at the travel agency. They are very well-matched in almost every possible way and enjoy a romantic love life.

Yet Oscar is haunted by memories of games he played with some friends at summer camp. From when they were twelve until about fourteen, they would spend a month at a summer sports camp in the mountains. At night, when most of the other campers and counselors were asleep, they would sneak out, tell each other "dirty stories" about their sexual fantasies, and touch themselves and each other "inappropriately." The "games" were consensual, and the stories were made up. Most of the boys, including Oscar, went on to date and fool around with girls into their teen years and beyond.

But Oscar has always felt very aware of, and even sometimes ashamed of, those nights. He has wondered if deep down he was really gay, even though all his love interests and fantasies were about women, and whenever he thought about dating or touching men, it didn't generate much interest or arousal. It was strange, because when one guy from the group came out in 11th grade, everyone, including Oscar, was totally supportive. It wasn't so much a fear about "being gay" as much as a constant wondering about whether he was, despite all evidence to the contrary.

There is another, deeper piece to this obsession: Oscar has always been an upstanding guy, even as a kid. Even though he was big and strong for his age, he never got into fights, bullied anyone, or even used intimidation. He had also been raised to be particularly respectful of women. Despite all this, he constantly worries about hurting others. While he knows that all the guys in their "group" had been willing participants, in the back of his mind he wonders and worries if those games made him a predator or a molester. He even went back at one point and asked some of the guys from camp if they remembered anyone being exploited, and they all recalled the games as open (if now embarrassing) play. Yet these thoughts and fears continue to pop up frequently and inconveniently, sometimes very randomly, and at other times, while he is touching Karen, wondering if she knows that deep down he is a "sexual deviant."

It was so important to Oscar to feel like a "good guy" rather than a "bad guy" that becoming a firefighter seemed almost like a natural choice for him—it gave him the possibility of being a hero instead of a villain. The rigorous training helped him feel a sense of control over his body, while his mind tormented him with shame and doubt. While he is quite balanced, healthy, happy, and self-disciplined in every other way, his mental preoccupation with his sexuality, safety, and moral standing causes him much anguish. As a result, he holds him back from really trusting himself with Karen and people in general.

<u>Oscar Revisited:</u>

Like Sophia, Oscar has also internalized a lot of unwarranted self- blame. On the one hand, he channeled his preoccupation with safety and being a "good guy" into choosing a career as a firefighter, a wonderful manifestation of the "hero complex." But on the other hand, he carries a backpack of shame and worry about what his childhood behavior meant. He has rewritten a relatively innocent story, and painted himself as a dangerous villain. He is also fixated on constantly questioning his sexuality in a way that negates his actual experiences. Here are Oscar's three narrative options:

1. *Below* **the Horizon:** "As a kid, I was big and strong and oversexual, and I acted out inappropriately with my friends. Sure, they say they liked it, but they were just kids—maybe I was really being pushy or abusive. Maybe I've been a pervert since childhood, and now maybe I'm really a sexual predator, just taking advantage of Karen's trust. If people knew what a sicko I really was, they would probably have me locked up."

Oscar is completely distorting his past and obsessing about his distortions, wasting precious mental energy doubting and disqualifying himself. Let's look at it from a lighter lens.

2. *On* **the Horizon:** "Ever since that experience with my buddies in camp, I've wondered about what that meant for me. I sensed there was something not right about it, even at the time. I know I've never purposely hurt anyone; that's the last thing I'd want to do. But I sometimes get these fears of being a danger to others. I also know I love Karen and feel very attracted to her. Yet I sometimes wonder if part of me could be gay. I try to remind myself that I'm living the life I want to be living, but these intrusive thoughts

can sometimes get me down. I think it's holding me back in certain ways."

Here, Oscar is acknowledging a more accurate version of his reality, while also attending to the problem of his fears and worries.

3. ***Above* the Horizon:** "Part of my sexual development included some fooling around with guys. As a kid I was confused and ashamed, and I think I processed it in two ways that aren't true for me today: one, thinking I'm gay, which would be fine, except that I'm not; and, two, thinking I'm a predator, which would not be ok, but fortunately that's not true either. When I'm in a calm place, my mind understands that I am who I am today, and that those thoughts really just come from a confused place in my past. I need to just remind myself that I am who I choose to be and enjoy the life and relationship I have today. Maybe if I talk to Karen about this, she will understand why I've been holding back somewhat and can also reassure me that she feels safe and fulfilled with me."

Go for it, Oscar!

Case Study: Sam's Selective Memory

Sam teaches a STEM enrichment program at an exclusive New England college prep school. He is in his mid-forties and aches to be a father. As the only child of elderly parents, he was loved and educated, given many opportunities, and pushed to achieve. But he had been lonely growing up and imagined one day having a lively house full of kids. Ever since he finished graduate school at twenty-five, he'd been dating women seriously with the hope of getting married and starting a family. For the past seven months, he's been seeing a colleague, a professor of literature at a nearby community college. They share a love of education and an appreciation for academia, sunsets, and aged wine. They've even enjoyed a week's vacation together, since their schedules coincided. For the first few months, Sam felt he'd finally found his match. They could talk for hours and never got bored.

But as the relationship progressed, Marci started to bring up philosophies about parenting. Sam understood that this was her way of trying to take the relationship deeper. He found his mind wandering, remembering past girlfriends and the things he liked about them. He noticed that Marci was far more reserved than Angela and Megan, two other women with whom he'd considered marriage. Angela used to laugh a lot—he'd loved to listen to her laugh. And Megan was always the life of the party— she had a magnetic personality. When he compared Marci to these women, she started to feel a little dull. He started to pull back a little in the relationship, and even when he was with her, he kept thinking about all the fun he'd had with Angela and Megan. Marci sensed his retreat, and finally told him she felt they were growing apart. She told him she had had high hopes for them as a couple, but that she really needed a guy who seemed more happy to be with her. Sam was grateful that he wasn't the one who had to end things.

What he didn't remember was that when Megan had brought up marriage, Sam had pulled away because he found her to be "overstimulating." And he had subconsciously pushed Angela away because once things got serious, he assessed her to be a bit of an "intellectual lightweight." As an intelligent, likeable man, there have been many women over the years who would have been thrilled to marry him. But when a relationship starts to get serious, Sam starts remembering the qualities of old flames that the current date is lacking. He romanticizes those women and/or their qualities in such a way that a live human could not possibly measure up.

Case Study Revisited: Sam

Sam's selective memory happens to be manifested in and compounded by an anxiety about commitment. While he was dating each woman, he initially enjoyed the positive qualities and experiences they brought to the relationships. But as he needed to zero in on making the leap into marriage, he found himself romanticizing past women and using those memories to disqualify and sabotage the current one. This is once again happening, this time with Marci. He is only remembering what was great about his past girlfriends and forgetting the downside of each one's temperament. We all have selective memories to a certain extent; we're not going to realistically remember everything in our lives accurately. But the key is to acknowledge the limitations of our mental memoirs and be aware when they are hindering our healthiness in the present and future.

1. *Below* **the Horizon:** "Whenever I spend time with Marci, I find myself remembering how much more fun I had with Angela and Megan. I guess that means something is missing from this connection."

If Sam could gain a little perspective about this tendency, it might sound like:

2. *On* **the Horizon:** "I know that when relationships start to get serious, I get nervous and start comparing the woman I'm with to women I've dated in the past. And I realize that those comparisons aren't really fair because I'm comparing the flaws in a current relationship with a rose-colored memory of a previous one."

That's where he notes the tendency. Here's where he adjusts it.

3. *Above* **the Horizon:** "For the last few months, I was so happy with Marci, and I never thought about other women. It was only when I started to think about commitment that I began comparing

her to idealized versions of old girlfriends. I realize that my fear of committing is probably causing my memory to concoct unfair competition for my relationship with Marci. This is my pattern. If I don't want to ruin this, I need to try and dismiss romanticized thoughts about Megan and Angela, and stay present enough with Marci to see if we can reconnect the way we have been until now."

Developing Healthy Narratives

If inaccurate mental memoirs are actually the norm, then how do we know when our memories are distorting our narratives in ways that are problematic, versus us simply editing naturally and adaptively over time?

Honestly, it can be hard to tell, sometimes. Generally, if the majority of the time you feel like an essentially happy, healthy, balanced, well-adjusted person in stable relationships with those around you, then your mind is probably doing a good enough job of filtering. But sometimes we can find ourselves plagued, distracted, or inhibited by varying forms of unpleasant, embellished, or interfering past-related thoughts. When that happens, it might be time to revisit and restructure past history and try to pull it *up to* or *above* the Horizon of Healthy Thinking.

We want to strive for balance. When we approach the events that brought us to where we are today, we don't want to catastrophize or over-blame past suffering, nor bask in illusions of past grandeur or perpetuate denial. Whether for bad, for good, or simply for drama, we want to ensure we are not making things bigger than they are, nor smaller than they are, and are just relating to them in reality. From there, we can figure out where we'd like to take ourselves. That is worth repeating in bold, so here goes: **Regardless of circumstances, we want to ensure we are not making things bigger than they are, nor smaller than they are. We want to relate to them as they are, or were, in reality. Then we want to figure out where we'd like to take ourselves afterwards.** This is a major key to healthy thinking and living, acceptance and action, and ultimately, personal fulfillment.

Not every mental memoir editing session will yield a definite or clear paradigm shift. The solutions are not always simple. But just the acts of taking a step back from the story we've been buying, challenging ourselves to imagine another possibility, and creating some distance from the problematic first draft are significant steps in the direction of healthier thinking and living. Even just getting to the Horizon, without lifting off to be above it, can make a difference in one's state of mind, if not in the plot itself.

Earlier, we discussed how residue from the past and fears about the future can crowd out the serenity of the present. In the next chapter, we're going to see how to apply the horizon method to looking ahead to the future.

CHAPTER 5:

And Now, Going Forward

My 18 year old son, Shmuel was once playing tennis on a court in a local park. A guy from the neighborhood, approached him and said: "You're really good- if you're ever looking for someone to practice with, please let me know." A couple of weeks later, Shmuel was looking for a tennis partner for the day, so I suggested he ask that fellow. Shmuel was hesitant, because he didn't that man so well, but I knew he very much wanted to play that day, so I encouraged him to speak to him. I said:

"Let's go through what could happen:

⇒ Option 1. He says: 'oh sure- what time can you meet?'

⇒ Option 2. He says: 'sorry- I'm not available today.'

⇒ Option 3. Worst case scenario, he says: 'Get out of my face, you moron- why would I want to play with you?'"

I was trying to be cute, but then Shmuel countered:

"No, worst case scenario, the guys reaches into his pocket, pulls out a gun, points it at me and says: 'You're gonna be sorry you asked me that!"

Of course, this was all in jest, but the truth is, we do tend to concoct some pretty outlandish worries about what could happen in the future.

Until now, we've been discussing different types of cognitive distortions of mental memoirs—rewriting events from past history—and how they can interfere with being healthy and happy in the present. We gave examples of how people have the possibility to challenge the limiting, unhelpful narratives and replace them with practical or empowering ones. Now let's focus on how the forward-thinking mind can either hold back, relate to, or enhance our life narratives.

A life-long gift from my mom:

I have a distinct childhood memory of walking out of a drug store with my mom, holding her hand, and asking her, "Which do you like better, being a kid or being an adult?" Her answer came without hesitation: "I like being an adult much better than being a kid. As an adult, there are so many more things you can do." In middle school, I remember complaining to her about the mean kids and the immature preteen social politics. I didn't understand the whole "getting mad at   " thing. My mom reassured me,   "This is a hard age; you'll see as you get older, you'll find more of 'your people.'" And she was right.

When I was pregnant with my first, my mom regaled me with stories of her wondrous experience of becoming a mom. But when I confided in her, as a new mom, how exhausted and overwhelmed I sometimes felt, she validated, "Yeah, they're so cute, but I'll never forget that profound exhaustion. As they get older, and you can really have a connection to them, talk to them, it gets better." And it did. When the toddlers committed their lives to trashing everything, mom said, "Yeah, you couldn't pay me to be 30 again. I enjoyed you guys so much more as you got older."

My mom gave me the gift of making whatever stage of life she was up to look awesome. She still does. She is a decidedly happy person. And because of that, no matter what hardships I was up to at a given stage of life, I felt like there was relief and a fun future around the bend. It helps me appreciate the joys of every stage and look forward to what comes next. If we recall the examples of past cognitive distortions of mental memoirs— **victimizing, denying, trivializing, exaggerating, self-blaming, obsessing, and selective memory**—it's not hard to see how those thought tendencies would manifest into the future, too.

1. When someone feels like a **victim** of past offenses, there often follows an expectation of

continuing to be beaten down by the same problems.

For example, "My boss low-balled my bonus this year because he's a misogynist," could easily lead to, "It's not worth even applying for that promotion; I know how he feels about women." Choosing to feel like a victim of sexism, rather than examining her profit and loss standing and objective compensation entitlement is holding this woman back from professional assertiveness and ambition.

A healthier version would be this: "I was disappointed with my holiday bonus this year. I need to look at my performance review and calculate what my work is worth. Based on that, I'll see if I can make a pitch for the promotion I've been eyeing. I'm not sure if my boss appreciates my contributions, but the only way to tell is by evaluating what I can do and applying for what I want. I hope this will get me where I want to be in my work, but if not, I can think about looking elsewhere to see if there's a better fit for me."

2. Those who deny, **trivialize, or exaggerate reality** as it was in the past are likely to deny, minimize, or inflate the potential obstacles or possibilities ahead.

For example, a person in denial might say, "My neighbor wasn't really using me when asked me to foot the entire bill for replacing the fence between our properties. It's just that he had just spent a lot of his rainy-day fund on a trip to Europe, so he's low on cash. It's easier for me to pay for it because I have more savings now. That's why I guess it's OK that I'll probably have to foot the bill for the cracked sidewalk repair in front of our houses, too." Denying that his neighbor was taking advantage of his generosity could set a precedent for further unfair financial arrangements between them.

A more direct acknowledgement of the situation could look like this: "My neighbor wasn't able to chip in for the fence we agreed to replace because he hadn't saved enough for it. I didn't mind laying out the cost for both of us because I had the money handy, and I like the guy. But we should establish a system for him to pay me back over time. Now that we'll need to tackle that sidewalk repair, it might be an opportunity for him to reciprocate by footing the bill, if he can. If not, maybe he can either take out a loan, or write up an official long-term payment plan, so I won't be out all this money indefinitely." By relating realistically to the imbalance in the initial arrangement, they can take steps toward more equitable sharing of expenses going forward, and maintain a more balanced approach to these costs.

One who exaggerates might say, "I remember when that kitchen contractor gave me a high estimate to replace my kitchen and said it was going to take a couple of months. I thought it was a rip-off, so I went to the home improvement store and bought the materials myself for a fraction of the cost. I did the whole job single-handedly in less than a week. It was so simple, and came out so great, that I think I might just open my own business doing low-cost kitchen renovation." An implausible and unrealistic memory of an amateur home repair could cause this individual to overestimate what she can accomplish for other homes and to take on irresponsible commitments that would land her in trouble.

A better representation of this could be: "I remember being discouraged by the proposal of a kitchen contractor for some updates we needed to do in our home. We ended up doing a lot of the work ourselves to save time and money. It was a lot of work, but I enjoyed it so much that I'm considering looking for work helping out on projects like this for other people. If it goes well, I would look into getting some vocational training in construction and seeing if that might be an option for a career change somewhere along the line." The unexaggerated version of this narrative would yield a more pragmatic and responsible take- away lesson for the future.

3.   If we **blame** ourselves unfairly for events of the past, this way of thinking might well hold us back from taking chances in the future, to avoid the pain of unwarranted guilt that can't be avoided.

For example, a person might think, "Last year, I tried to take my parents out for dinner in honor of their anniversary. But my dad had a bad slip and fall in the lobby of the restaurant and has been in painful physical therapy for months. I've felt so awful about it, I refuse to take them out in public again; I don't want to be responsible for either of them getting injured again." By taking on personal blame for a complete accident, he is depriving himself and his parents of the pleasure of future outings together.

Here's a healthier way to process this event: "Last time I took my parents out, I had really wanted them to have a fun celebratory dinner, but it ended so badly. It was scary and upsetting to see Dad hurt like that. I know the fall was mostly just bad luck, but I realize my parents are getting older, and I want to be sure they can handle the plans we make together. Next time I want to take them out, maybe I'll check with his doctor to make sure he's up to it and see if there are any precautions I can take to be as safe as reasonably possible." This version addresses the past mishap and the desire to learn from it, if possible, without assuming personal blame for a common, maybe even inevitable, accident.

4.   **Obsession** about problems that have not yet presented themselves, or the epidemic of "what ifs," is another way our futures paralyze us.

Someone might think, "Ever since I saw that documentary about a plane crash a few years ago, I've been absolutely terrified to fly. It's gotten so I'll opt for a thirty-hour road trip to avoid a three- hour flight, even if it means missing days of work. It comes up a lot because I often need to travel for work, and because my family lives all over the country, so whenever anyone is flying anywhere, I literally don't sleep until I know they've landed safely." A preoccupation with the unlikely danger of flying is inhibiting this person from normal travel options and peace of mind. These fears can morph into phobias or debilitating obsessions if they go unchecked.

Here is one possible alternative: "Ever since I saw that scary movie, it's like I have this bug in my head, and I've found that I've become genuinely scared of flying. I imagine that the more I avoid it, the more the fear can grow and significantly interfere with my life. I want to face the fear head-on, so I'm going to try to challenge myself to take a short flight to visit my brother over Thanksgiving weekend. I hope that by pushing through it, I will be able to conquer it. But if not, I'll speak to a counselor and try to get some tools to regain my courage. Travel is too much a part of my life to allow fear to limit me this way." See how the difference between obsessing about the danger vs. committing to work through the fear can make a real difference in how the future narrative plays out?

5. **Selective memory** about past experiences can also create inaccurate assessments about future situations.

A person might say, "I know I have a lot on my plate right now, but I remember last time I trained for the marathon, it wasn't such a big deal; all I did was go running on the promenade with my cousin for an hour once a week for a couple of months, and then I was totally in shape and ready in time" ...forgetting about the dozens of hours spent on the treadmill at the gym near work and the still-tender ankle break a few months afterwards.

A more accurate memory would be, "I remember how much I enjoyed training for and running the marathon a few years ago. I have a lot more going on in my life right now, and I've hurt myself since then, but I'd still love to see if I can figure out a way to run again. I should research how to pace myself, train, manage time, and not strain my ankle too much. If I can make this work with my schedule and my body, that would be great. But if not, maybe some light jogging on the promenade with my cousin again every week would be a good start for now."

Fear of Failure

I think the majority of us underestimate and underachieve for the future because of a fear of failure. I have clients who are afraid to get too intimate with a partner because of all the risk entailed:

- "What if I get hurt?"
- "What if I break someone's heart?"
- "What if it all doesn't work out in the end?"
- "What if there's someone better for me out there?"

Fears around having a baby:

- "What if something goes wrong with the pregnancy?"

- "What if the baby isn't well?"
- "What if I can't handle labor and delivery?"
- "What if I'm a terrible parent and ruin my child forever?"
- "What if I don't like my kids? Or they don't like me?"

Fears around applying for higher education or for a better job:

- "What if I get rejected?"
- "What if I can't keep up with the demands?"
- "What if I end up hating this work and trapped in a miserable job?"
- "What if I flop financially?"

Fears around confiding in a friend:

- "What if I get judged, misunderstood, or betrayed?"
- "What if I regret sharing and it comes back to bite me?"
- "What if they don't see me the same way after this?"
- "What if they tell others or distort what I say?"

Fears around public speaking:

- "What if I freeze up and forget everything I want to say?"
- "What if I stutter, mess up, or get heckled?"
- "What if they hate what I have to say?"
- "What if my lecture gets posted online and shredded by critics?"

The lists can go on and on. Any point of decision-making is an opportunity for self-doubt and fear. All of those what-ifs are technically possible. But we can "what-if" our way into analysis paralysis if we go all the way with that kind of thinking. We all do here and there, but the trick is to not let it become a deterrent to leading the lives we want to lead, to not let it hold us back from taking chances toward self-actualization.

Once, when I was a little kid, my father took us ice skating. My brother kept trying fancy tricks and showing off, while I kept skating around the rink in rhythmic, deliberate circles. My brother kept falling, and being an insufferably snooty older sister, I pointed out to my dad, "He keeps falling, but I haven't fallen once yet." My dad wisely explained, "Yes, you're not falling, but that's because you're taking the safe path. You're skating OK, but you're not trying anything different or learning anything new. He is trying to challenge himself to do harder things on the ice. That's why he's falling, but that's how he'll get better as a skater, too." True story, Dad.

I know that I've been wanting to write a book since I was a kid, but a combination of fear of failure and poor organizational skills and time management held me back. Fear of failure can manifest in different ways. It can look like anxiety, lack of confidence, lack of time, or lack of focus. But a belief in the value of trying, even without guaranteed results, can redirect us from the pressure to succeed.

CHAPTER 6:

And Speaking of Books

<u>**My Love of Bibliotherapy**</u>

Confession: I am a lifelong bibliophile. That's not as creepy as it sounds- it just means that I love books. (And not just because they were my only friends in the fourth grade.) Most contemporary self-help books and articles include a caveat such as, "No book or article can take the place of a trained professional—if you have a problem, seek help from a reputable, licensed clinician." I don't disagree with that, especially when it comes to severe pathology. But the truth is, for many of us, books can make a pretty amazing adjunct to good therapy. And for the many, many individuals whose problems are not severe or disruptive enough to warrant seeking professional help in their own estimation, books are a fabulous resource. One of my more annoying qualities as a therapist is the tendency to recommend too many books. I don't want to overwhelm my clients, but there are several reasons why I strongly recommend reading between sessions.

1.   **Honesty**: I'm grateful to have a practice where I can charge privately by the hour, but I don't

want to be a rip-off. If I know that clients could spend an afternoon reading a $12 book and learn tools that would take me a few hundred dollars' worth of sessions to teach them, it just feels wrong not to offer that option.

2. **Potency**: Coming to the office once a week or so will offer an experience to talk and learn, but it's somewhat isolated from the other areas of life. Bringing self-help materials into the home, in real time and space, blends an organic continuity to the healthy messages we're trying to internalize.

3. **Variety**: Interacting with one therapist is helpful, but it's one- dimensional exposure. Integrating a more diverse group of authors and voices, reverberating their own permutations and harmonies to the work in other contexts, adds a sort of surround-sound quality to the messages.

4. **Autonomy**: I generally favor brief therapy. I don't want clients to feel dependent on a therapist for skills and information. Encouraging reading is sort of like the homeschooling of counseling. When people see and feel how inspired and empowered they can become just by reading someone else's words, they become more courageous and ready to manage their challenges independently. Of course, I don't kick people out of therapy prematurely, and I'm still always here if they want to come back for a

"tune-up" visit, but the goal is usually self-sufficiency.

5.   **In lieu:** There are many, many individuals who are going through personal situations or struggling with past or future "stuff" but don't actually require clinical intervention. They are stable, functional, and mostly happy. But they want to work on themselves in some way or gain insight. For those consumers, a good self-improvement book can be a fabulous catalyst for growth.

Of course, if clients prefer not to read and only want to attend sessions, that's fine, too. But I see that clients who are willing and able to read between sessions often move more quickly and efficiently through the therapy process, and can get more out of the sessions, too. For those who hate to read, or who don't have time, I also recommend audiobooks and lectures for driving time, exercise, or during housework—whatever way possible to make use of the plethora of information available. Then again, if you're already up to this point in my book, I'm probably preaching to the choir...

The next natural question would be, "Ok, Elisheva, I'm getting the feeling that you're a proponent of bibliotherapy. But what should I read?"

I'm so glad you pretend-asked.

Every so often, maybe once every couple of years, I'll read a book and then say to myself, "Now I need to go ahead and read every book this person wrote." My UPS delivery guy calls me his favorite bookaholic. Because I view books as such a rich and powerful medium for personal development, I would like to share a partial selection of some of my favorite authors with you, and what I learned from them, specifically with regards to the Horizon technique.

Healthy Perspectives and Implementations of Time Management

What is the most valuable, nonrenewable resource we have? That would probably be time. Time is the canvas on to which we design our lives, the protoplasm in which all other functions subsist. Naturally, it would be worthwhile to strategize about how we want to best utilize this precious gift, our limited years on this planet, to actualize most effectively and authentically.

Laura Vanderkam

I was introduced to Laura's work by a wonderful client of mine. Laura has conducted extensive research exploring working moms and time management; she explains obvious facts in a user- friendly, motivating way.

The premise: We all have the same 168 hours in our week. Even if we sleep eight hours a night and work 40 hours a week, that still leaves 72 hours weekly to be used at our discretion. In one powerful exercise, she asked participants to use a sheet with 336 squares to represent the number of 30-minute slots we each have in our week. She had them fill in, every 30 minutes, what they had just been doing for the last half-hour. This included sleeping, showering, eating, exercising, chatting, relaxing, various types of online activity, housekeeping—everything got logged, so that by the end of the week they could track every single 30-minute slot of their lives for that week and how it was spent.

After a couple of weeks doing that, the participants analyzed how they spent their time and realized that they tended to be pretty inaccurate in their approximations of how they thought they allocated their hours. The next phase of the exercise was to *prescribe in advance*, rather than just describe, how they intended to spend their boxes. Every night, or at the beginning of the week, participants would fill in their squares the way they hoped to spend their time.

The results were that these people found that when they looked at their weeks as blank slates' worth of potential time, and planned in advance what they wanted to do, they were able to utilize their time far more efficiently and gratifyingly. There is a huge difference between looking up after browsing on Amazon for an hour and saying, "Gee, where did that hour go?" versus deliberately penciling in a daily allowance for online shopping and browsing.

Here are several of her most popular books: *168 Hours: You Have More Time Than You Think; I Know How She Does It: How Successful Women Make the Most of Their Time; and What the Most Successful People Do Before Breakfast*. They have proven to be an exceptionally worthwhile investment of my own time, and that of many of my clients.

Preemptive Troubleshooting

When I recommend Laura's books and exercises to my clients and supervisees, their automatic response is generally, "Well, that's all well and good for someone with a predictable life and schedule. But I get all kinds of interruptions and detours over the course of my day: a kid sent home from school with strep, an emergency at the warehouse, a flat tire. I can't anticipate these things and then my whole plan will get derailed." But remember, Laura's research was specifically conducted with working moms—these are very busy people with very unpredictable lives. The goal is not to stick rigidly to the plan; the goal is to start with an optimal plan in place, which is, of course, subject to change as unforeseeable events come up. There is a world of difference between just going through our day or week hand-to-mouth, putting out fires and wasting time, versus having a clear plan and itinerary with built-in flexibility and the ability to make necessary adjustments as needed. It also makes it easier to come back to tasks that got sidelined when we know exactly what supplanted them and why.

Another resistance I encounter when introducing Laura's approach is, "I feel like the idea of having to account for every minute of my day will stress me out. I don't work like that; I need downtime to just chill, be creative, or not have anything at all to do." Well, my response to that (as I imagine Laura's is) is if your current system was working out well for you, we probably wouldn't be discussing this. And, being proactive and organized about time management doesn't have to mean being uptight and overzealous. On the contrary, if you know you like some downtime after work, or on the weekends, figure out about how much of that you want. Pencil in all the things that *have* to happen, all the things you want to do or accomplish, all the recreational fun you want to make time for, and then what you have left you could allocate for "chill time." And because everything else got assigned, your chill time is guilt-free.

I would love to say that after reading Laura's works, I always use my spreadsheets to track and plan my hours. Alas, I don't (yet) have that level of self-discipline. But it has altered the way I plan my days and weeks, and dramatically improved my time management. Most meaningfully, it gave me the confidence to decide that I didn't need to choose between homeschooling my children and my 6 figure private practice. By organizing my time and priorities proactively, I've been able to fit both in, and still have time to read, write, and recreate. (Caveat: I do neglect housework, but have learned to delegate that.)

Matthew Kelly

Matthew has a beautifully clear, understandable, and readable writing style and message. Each of his books is a manual designed to help readers in their quests to become, to quote his mantra, "the best possible versions of ourselves." He predicates much of his theory on the fundamental quadrants of *mind, body, heart,* and *soul,* urging readers to nurture themselves and their relationships intellectually, physically, emotionally, and spiritually. He gives wonderful guidance, anecdotes, and advice on how to do just that.

The first book I heard about was The Seven Levels of Intimacy: *The Art of Loving and the Joy of Being Loved.* This (along with Gary Chapman's *The Five Love Languages*), has since become nearly standard recommended reading for any couple I treat for relationship goals. Matthew describes intimacy as the mutual and ongoing process of revealing oneself to another, in increasingly deep ways, in the presence of acceptance and caring. He breaks down different levels of trust and revelation into phases, ranging from most superficial to more intimate and vulnerable: clichés; facts; opinions; hopes and dreams; feelings; fears, faults, and failures; and legitimate needs. He describes the importance of connecting with our primary love relationship, as well as other close ones, in deep and intimate ways, rather than just relying on the chit-chat of the first three levels to maintain shallow connection. This is the recipe for love—being known, understood, and valued, and then doing the same thing right back.

After the *Seven Levels*, I read the *Rhythm of Life: Living Every Day with Passion and Purpose*, a book about balance, fulfillment, and making good life choices. I found it so motivating and uplifting that once I finished it, I invited my then-15-year-old son to read it together with me as a springboard for discussion and bonding in small daily doses. We finished it over about seven months and grew closer together through it. I also appreciated Matthew's book, *Building Better Families: A Practical Guide to Raising Amazing Children*, so much that I downloaded it onto my iPhone as an audiobook, and we listened to it as a group on a family road trip in Arizona one summer.

Brené Brown

Brené has taken the mental health world by storm over the past decade. Her book, *The Gifts of Imperfection*, is an entertaining, touching, enlightening journey of her own life lessons toward wholehearted living. Her subsequent works, *I Thought It Was Just Me (But It Isn't)*, *Daring Greatly*, *Rising Strong*, and *Braving the Wilderness*, are a deeper continuation of her magnificent message—the condition of being human, the inherent shame we need to work through to find the courage to be authentic, and the joys and struggles inherent in that process. A gifted storyteller, honest researcher, powerful spokesperson, and refreshing human being, Brené is a treat to know through her writing.

I have not (yet) had the privilege to meet Brené in person, but I can say that if not for her, I doubt I would have found the courage to publish. Thanks, hon! (It would be so cool if she read that..)

Richard Carlson

When I was kid, my friends would sometimes go with their parents to work, or bring home various tchotchkes from their offices. My dad is a psychologist in private practice, so there were no "hang out at dad's office" days or free memorabilia. But I finally got my perk when I went into the mental health field and found that he was, and is, a wealth of wisdom, life experience, and professional expertise, at my fingertips. To this day, we share a love of books, trading titles and reviews on each visit.

Early on in my own practice, he recommended a book called *You Can Feel Good Again*, by Richard Carlson, as supplementary material for treating depression. I was so enamored with the book that I based two support groups I was running at that time entirely on that content. My only critique of that book is that I wish it weren't written only for depression—the ideas and techniques are so rich and valuable that they can be applied to any form of toxic thinking. Much of the basis for the Horizon of Healthy Thinking was born as a result of reading that book.

More gems by *Carlson include the popular Don't Sweat the Small Stuff series* and *Slowing Down to the Speed of Life*, co-authored with Joseph Bailey, also about using the mind to take perspective for healthier living.

Neil Pasricha

If laughter is the best medicine, then Neil Pasricha has made a real contribution to the area of wellness. His *The Book of Awesome* is a laugh-out-loud book with a great backstory. Neil was at a low point in his life—a failed marriage, a floundering career, a sense of hopelessness, battling depression. He decided to try and cheer himself up by starting a playful gratitude blog called, "1000 Awesome Things." He challenged himself to find one thing each day that he could call "awesome," mostly minutia, like the fun of popping bubble wrap or watching milk swirl into coffee.

This began as a form of personal amusement, which he originally shared with his parents just for fun. But his gift for humor and writing, along with his honesty and earthiness, touched the hearts of his readers and catapulted him into the spotlight. He subsequently went back to school, got a degree, produced a popular TED talk, and then went on to research and write a more serious book on the subject of happiness called *The Happiness Equation,* which I also heartily recommend.

CHAPTER 7:

Values, Morality, Religion, Dogma, and Doctrine

Growing up and living in a very religious subculture, I wanted to include a chapter that reflected my existential struggles and musings in a way that would also feel relevant to the many readers who do not identify themselves as religious. I realized that while my particular exposure to ethical development was flavored predominantly by religious concepts and language, almost everyone evolves in some context of "should/should not" thinking. Thinking, speaking, and writing about right/wrong binary judgements is a challenge, and I do so with some apprehension, but here goes:

Values and dogma present a challenge in terms of Horizon thinking. Because we may be thinking or expressing ourselves from a position we view as objectively "right," we might feel justified in dipping below the Horizon into a place of superiority, without even realizing it. (I know I do this *all* the time. As a little girl, my parents used to call me the walking superego.) Remember: *below* the Horizon thinking just means unproductive or unhealthy, not necessarily inferior. Being judgmental, superior, condescending, or arrogant can actually feel pretty good at the time. But that doesn't make it healthy or helpful.

Extremist, radical religion has long been criticized for dogma and intolerance, and continues to be called out on this problem. Contemporary Western society has evolved its own equivalent, secularly adapted, humanistic moral barometer for judgment. Staunch far-leftist ideology, especially in university, media, and celebrity cultures, has taken on a sort of religious zealotry; for example, extreme political correctness and social justice.

Almost all of us have values—some innate, others learned or acquired and invariably tweaked over time. Some are lofty and theological or philosophical, while others are more practical, interpersonal, survival- or achievement-based. Some people naturally lead lives that are harmonious with their own values, while others grapple, fake, rationalize, or cheat. Some people think and talk more about these ideals and rules, while others simply practice or ignore them, until something glaring arises.

In the Yeshiva schools where I studied (and taught), and at the adult lectures I attend (and give), I've experienced different styles of conveying values-based ideology, styles which I've come to notice are fairly universal for education with a moral agenda. I call them the four "I's" of influence: information, inspiration, indoctrination, and intimidation.

- **Information**: This is my favorite form of education because it feels the most intellectually honest and shows the most respect for the audience. Information involves relaying facts, primary sources, and rationales for analysis by intelligent minds.

- **Inspiration**: This form of education involves an emotional appeal and can be motivating and uplifting. It could be in the form of stories, poetry, music, media, or encouragement. Inspiration, to my mind, is best utilized as seasoning for information. We wouldn't recommend a steady diet of only herbs and spices, but using judicious amounts of inspiration to flavor and propel effective use of information is like applying proportionate amounts of seasoning to a nutritious meal.

- **Indoctrination**: This form of education is the emphatic, repetitive, dogmatic assertion of agenda-based material using strong, persuasive language. An excellent example of indoctrination-style teaching would be the following. My teenage son and his friends asked a certain Rabbi-teacher what the Judaic perspective would be with regard to Jews observing a specific patriotic ritual. The Rabbi replied, "Well, have you done it until now?" and the boys replied that they had not. His response was, "Well then, you've gotten this far without it, clearly it's not that important." He considered the question answered, but fortunately my son and his friends were astute enough to realize it wasn't, and went on to ask another Rabbi-teacher (who told them that it is, indeed, a Jewish value to show respect to the country in which you live).

- **Intimidation**: Moral intimidation is the use of pejorative words, volume, degradation, or threat of punishment to invoke agreement, obedience, or at the very least, silence.

To illustrate these different styles of influence, we can look at a particular value through each lens. Many idealistic communities are wary of the dangers of internet abuse. Here are some ways they could try to influence their constituents to proceed with caution.

- **Information**: Sharing tools, websites, research, and training about responsible internet use, parental supervision, family filters, and personal accountability. Sharing ideas to help learners utilize online resources without getting hooked on screens or seduced by the illegal, dangerous, or harmful online sites or predators. This information could include data and statistics about internet addiction, pedophilia, pornography, hackers, identity theft, exploitation, traps, scams, sites to avoid, and ways to be a safe and savvy consumer.
- **Inspiration**: Stories about families and individuals who limit screen time, make time to "unplug" and how beneficial it has been for them personally. Opinions about how important it is to look up from

our phones and laptops, get some fresh air, interact live, exercise, have experiences, and do things in real life rather than virtually. Examples of parents who limit or restrict their families' internet access, and how pure, innocent, happy, healthy, and wholesome they are relative to their peers.

- **Indoctrination**: Telling kids and families that the internet has no place in a healthy, religious home. That it promotes a false and distorted picture of reality, seduces users away from their best selves, wastes valuable time and energy, and leads to addiction and moral disintegration. That generations of good, moral people have raised strong, hard-working families by engaging in real-life interactions, and that the technological revolution is a dangerous experiment from which no good can come. We'd best stay far, far away.

- **Intimidation**: Preaching that internet use is sinful and idolatrous, the work of the devil or Satan. That children who have online access will likely end up in the clutches of predators or stalkers. Their innocence will be ripped away, and their lives will be ruined. Adults who use the internet will become glazed, distracted, irresponsible, promiscuous, and naturally, end up in Hell.

While these examples are admittedly a bit extreme, so are many other of the agenda-based messages out there. Just listen to the debates about political hot-button topics such as gun laws, abortion, or immigration policies. Real, honest dialogue takes place in the realm of information seasoned judiciously by inspiration. Once extreme views and personalities join the fray, the indoctrination and intimidation take over, and it's much harder to get things under control again, regardless of the issue at hand.

A Word About Hypocrisy

Hypocrisy is a word that, in my opinion, gets grossly overused, and tends to be an inaccurate, unhelpful way of categorizing people or deeds. Acting in a way that is not necessarily in harmony with one's beliefs does not make someone a hypocrite— it makes them human. Every person at some time or another will let himself down, fail to live up to his own standard, or mess up— in both big and little ways.

Here is the difference. Let's say I teach my children not to speak ill of others, which is both a religious and a humanistic value, and then one day they hear me speaking disparagingly about someone else. One of them says to me, "Mom, what you just said—isn't that the kind of thing you tell us not to say?" If my response is, "Excuse me, I'm the adult here, I can say what I want; you just do as you're told and follow the rules," that will be experienced as hypocritical—I'm not practicing what I preach, and I'm telling them to do as I say, but not as I do. No one likes or respects a phony.

On the other hand, if my response is, "Actually, now that you mention it, you're 100% right. I didn't agree with what that man said, but I could have expressed my opinion more respectfully. Thanks for pointing that out. I apologize for speaking that way, and I'm going to be more careful." What I'm conveying here is that I made a mistake, I admit and regret it and intend to do better going forward. Modeling acceptance of our own imperfections is a great statement to those around us. It shows we are sincere, trustworthy, humble, and growth-oriented. But most importantly, it imprints that message within our own hearts, strengthening our character going forward. That is the opposite of hypocritical.

Phony vs. Polite

Years ago, I was teaching in a local high school, and having a discussion with a group of adolescent girls. We were discussing the issue of cliques and snobbery among their grade. I told the kids that I felt a worthwhile goal would be that any student could smile or greet any other student in the school for no other reason than they crossed paths and made eye contact, even if they weren't acquainted. I had suggested a program called Greeting Day, where the goal was to encourage everyone to make a point of greeting each other on that day and reciprocate in kind, breaking down social barriers and connecting.

One of the girls objected to the idea, saying she thought it all sounded very fake. "I just don't get the point. If I don't know someone, and I don't care about her, or I don't like him, wouldn't saying good morning or smiling just be fake? I don't want to be a phony." Some of the other kids agreed.

I was surprised that such an innocuous, ostensibly feel-good suggestion could be perceived as controversial. I tried to explain the difference: "If you say hi to someone that you generally ignore because you want to ask her a favor, that might be fake. Or, if you smile warmly, and then immediately turn around and roll your eyes or make a mean comment—also fake. But, if you greet someone you don't know or care for because you are trying to be a kinder, more respectful person, because you are trying to make another person smile and you genuinely believe that's a valuable thing to do, that's called being nice or polite."

The Talmud has a fascinating take on this practice: "One should always engage in good deeds, even for the wrong reasons, because *from the midst of the ulterior, comes the altruistic." Tractate Pesachim, p. 50.*

I gave these teens an example of this. "Let's a say a kid in your class asks if you want to study for a math test together. You don't particularly want to study with her, and anyway, your math skills are stronger than hers, so you'd essentially be helping her study. But then you remember that she has an incredibly cute, popular, and athletic older brother, whom you'd like to get to know. So you agree to meet at her house after school. You're not agreeing for the right reasons, but in the end, you study with her, and you do a good thing. It's entirely possible that you will end up enjoying spending time with this classmate and making a real friend out of it, despite going just for her brother the first time, and then you hang out for fun. Or you might enjoy the feeling you get from helping someone out so much that you end up helping other people study, too, even without a cute older brother. From the ulterior to the altruistic."

Phony or fake means being maliciously deceptive. Being nice, even if you don't feel like it, is just being a kind person. What's the difference between hypocritical and imperfect, or phony and polite? Just that Horizon of Healthy Function and the way it plays out in our behavior and self-image. The story we write.

Guilt vs. Gratitude

During the summer, my daughter, Sussy, was assigned some books to read in preparation for her 9th grade literature course. One of the books was a beautiful memoir called *I Will Always Write Back,* by Caitlin Alifirenka and Martin Ganda. It is the true story of two teenagers, the authors, who live across the world from one another and are connected through a school-based pen pal program: a suburban middle schooler from Pennsylvania who enjoys trips to the mall and fleeting crushes; and an impoverished, brilliant teen from Zimbabwe who sleeps on a crowded dirt floor in a shared hut, eats rationed coarse grains for his meals, and must leave school whenever his family can't afford to pay the tuition bill. Caitlin ends up getting involved and helping Martin pursue his educational goals and break the cycle of poverty in his family. It was a fabulous assignment for the students in our upper-middle class community, a real glimpse into a world beyond our first world privilege.

Sussy, a thoughtful, sensitive soul, was sharing the story with me while we were standing in Target, carefully deliberating between a package of Kit Kat or Twix for nourishment on our plane ride to the Grand Canyon.

"I feel like it's important for me to read this book; it's really changing my understanding of what goes on in the world, and especially in places like North Africa. But it also makes me feel kind of guilty. Like here I am, with a whole room full of my own stuff—books, games, clothes, even my own cell phone—and I feel bad about enjoying all this when there are kids my age all over the world who don't even have a bed or healthy food to eat." I was grateful that Sussy was so honest about her reaction, because it was a terrific opportunity for us to discuss the difference between guilt and gratitude, something that many adults confuse, particularly when it comes to socioeconomic privilege.

I told her something like the following: "I really relate to the idea of feeling guilty to be a 'have' in a world with so much 'have not.' But I don't think that feeling guilty about the gifts we've been blessed with is going to make the world better. I think a healthier response is two-fold:

1. Appreciate and enjoy what we have. To have plenty of food, a comfortable, safe home, running water, electricity, internet, and educational opportunities is both a blessing and a responsibility. Take note of these things daily and give thanks where it's due.

2. Realize, empathize, and appreciate that not everyone has these things and think about what we can do to make a difference. The girl in the book dedicated time, effort, and her babysitting money to help a friend in real need. She, and eventually her family, made a huge difference in the life of this boy and his family. Our family regularly donates a percentage of our income and our gently used clothes to charity. You give of your time to local families in need, tutoring, babysitting, and visiting the elderly. But maybe we can look into ways to help people in need in other parts of the globe, too."

Helping Sussy shift from guilt to gratitude and generosity was a great exercise in Horizon thinking:

1. ***Below*** **the Horizon:** "I feel like a shallow, spoiled brat when I read about poor people in developing countries. And it's so depressing how hard it is out there for some people."

2. ***On*** **the Horizon:** "Learning about extreme poverty was a reality check, and it kind of makes me feel uncomfortable with our own abundance, which I realize I probably take for granted."

3. ***Above*** **the Horizon:** "Reading a book like this makes me realize my good fortune at being born into a country and family with so much comfort, safety, and opportunity. It also inspires me to try and figure out ways that I can help share these blessings with others who are less fortunate."

On a less profound note, Sussy's story reminded me of a personal discovery I made a few years ago. I was talking with a close friend about the fact that I don't enjoy receiving material gifts. I had always thought it was because I have an issue with managing clutter and that I'm not good at choosing gifts to reciprocate. But once we really got to analyzing it, I realized that it's also that I'm uncomfortable with the sense of beholdenness that comes along with receiving. For some reason, I equate receiving with "owing." I'm not really sure why or how my personality evolved that way; I don't love taking favors either, so it's consistent with my personality. My parents have always been giving, but not overindulgent by comparison to my peers'.

Whatever the origins, realizing that receiving was being processed unhelpfully by my mind allowed me to work on rescripting my reactions to gifts. Instead of my internal narration to getting something being, "I feel so bad that they went to the trouble/expense… it wasn't necessary… you shouldn't have," I have been trying to consciously shift toward a more gracious and grateful response along the lines of, "How kind and thoughtful of them! What a lovely gesture…. I feel so cared for… I look forward to being able to get or do the same for them or someone else sometime." It was as though I went from feeling apologetic to feeling appreciative and expansive.

This shift also allows me to give to others in a more comfortable way. I think I used to project my own discomfort with receiving onto my recipients. When they would thank me, I would shrink inwards and trivialize by saying things like, "It's just a little something… I wasn't sure if it's your taste… It's no big deal… I was going anyway… It's the least I could do." One day, a friend dropped off a lovely gift for my son. When I thanked her profusely, she flashed me a warm smile and simply replied, "You're very welcome—I hope he enjoys it." Then she waved goodbye, hopped into her car and drove off. So simple, but so not the way I was accustomed to giving. Seeing her give in such a genuine, uncomplicated way inspired me to try and do the same. No apologies, explanations, or commentary—just, "Here, I hope you enjoy it. Have a great day!"

I also realized that I tended to overthink gifts—it shouldn't be too chintzy or too showy, it should be appropriate for the recipient and the occasion, but not something everyone else with think to give. How exhausting! Of course, I want to be thoughtful, timely, and personal in choosing gifts. But now that I've shifted my thinking, once I've chosen something, it's time to write a card, drop it off, and be done with it. Sometimes, I remind myself how I feel when I receive a gift that's not my taste. After expressing appropriate thanks, I just think, "Oh, that was thoughtful of them, even though it happens to not be my taste." And then somehow, life goes on. Remembering that is a good antidote for my gifting anxiety. Gratitude, not guilt. Sometimes I need to repeat it in my head a few times, but at least I know what the goal is.

Dealing with Feelings

There has been an increased emphasis on feelings over the course of my lifetime. In the religious schools I attended growing up, we were often taught that feelings were a sort of weakness and that the logical should always trump the emotional. Then- switcheroo- at my liberal college and grad schools, we were taught to embrace the motley, if fickle and subjective, world of emotional experience. Honestly, neither of them ultimately resonated with me as healthy. As with most other polarized positions, there tends to be a happy medium.

Invalidating feelings—our own or anyone else's—is untruthful, unkind, and unproductive. Squelching the way we feel in favor of the way we *want* to feel or the way we think *others* want us to feel ends up making us feel disconnected from ourselves. Disqualifying the feelings of others is tactless and uncaring, and disconnects us from both others and our own authentic selves.

At the other extreme, over-identifying with feelings is dangerous. If we buy into the caprice of emotion at all times, we can become unstable and unfocused. We become like chaff in the wind, blowing wherever our hormones take us. If we over-empathize with others' feelings, we can lose ourselves in their drama or in the relationship.

Some people tend toward the first extreme, either repressing or ignoring their own feelings and/or the feelings of others. Those people will sometimes feel empty or detached, and often want to learn how to access their own feelings and/or relate to the feelings of others. Other folks tend toward the opposite pole, easily becoming flooded by emotion, both theirs or others'. Those individuals may reach a point where they are suffering from the "noise" of it all and want to learn how to calibrate or boundary themselves.

There are also some of us who waffle between the tendencies. I know that I have the capacity to become flooded by both my own and others' emotional experiences. Maybe even due to that, I also have a tendency to sometimes turn away, instinctively, from feeling my own feelings or those of others. The key, as always, is balance.

In the *mind-body-heart-soul* quadrants, I believe mind and soul should be the leaders, and the body and heart should be the followers. What does that look like? The mind tells us what is logical and practical. The soul tells us what is right, good, and true, and what is not. The body tells us what feels good physically, and the heart tells us what feels good or bad emotionally.

If we listened only to our bodies, we would eat whatever tastes good and do whatever feels good, as far as physical pleasures. These may not be healthy choices, but the body is not naturally responsible or practical. In order to manage our bodies well, we need to harness the power of our minds and souls. When the body says it wants junk food and sleep, the mind says it needs nourishing food and exercise. When the body wants immediate sex with anyone that's available, the soul says it should be discerning and self-respecting, and wants us to practice safe, moral sex with safe, consensual partners.

If we listened only to our hearts, we would do things only when in the mood, and avoid anything that didn't immediately gratify us. I would only return the calls that I felt like returning or honor the commitments I enjoyed. If I woke up not in the mood to go to work or care for my children, I would "follow my heart," listen to my feelings, and just do what I want. When the mind and the soul weigh in, they tell me that it makes no sense to blow off work (illogical and irresponsible), and it's not right to neglect my kids (immoral and selfish). My heart never wants to say no to requested favors or do anything that will make my children sad. My mind reminds me of the importance of boundaries in relationships and the responsibility to take the kids to the dentist.

Our hearts and feelings can help us understand the thought processes in our minds and experience life richly and in living color. They can help us empathize with others and be gentle with ourselves. But in the end, they make poor masters. Feelings are like the children of our inner selves. Children are beautiful, innocent, honest, and lovely. They are repositories of vast potential, creativity, and light. But they are also often unpredictable, self-absorbed, erratic, distractible, and irrational. They can't be trusted for important decisions, but their needs must be acknowledged, measured, honored, and treated with care.

Of course, the quadrants intersect. For example, it may be perfectly honest to make a true, but tactless comment to another individual. But the heart may feel that it's not kind because it will make both the speaker and listener feel bad. The mind will say it's not a smart thing to do because hurting the feelings of another person will harm friendships. And the soul may argue that it's morally wrong to cause another emotional pain. So the mind and the soul consult with the expertise of the heart to make a choice that makes moral, intellectual, and emotional sense.

To my clients (and kids and friends and self) who can get overtaken by emotion, the mantra I offer is: *Don't take your feelings too seriously.* I know that sounds like a funny thing for a therapist to say. And it's not always the appropriate advice for everyone. But for many of us, we can get caught up in the difference between, "I am angry," and "I feel angry." It's better to remember that feelings come and go, but facts, values, beliefs, and morals tend to serve us in better stead.

But What About the Heavy Stuff?

The other day I was listening to a recording of Dennis Prager interviewing a writer by the name of Rabbi Steve Leder. They were discussing his book, *More Beautiful than Before: How Suffering Transforms Us*, in which he tackles the infinitely difficult subject of the innocent suffering. The good rabbi tells Dennis that he has counseled so many parents who've lost children that he's lost count of the number, but he remembers all of them.

I've heard many different thinkers talk about grief, but what struck me about Rabbi Leder's tone and approach was the magnificent synthesis of empathy, realism, acceptance, and faith.

Some speakers sound too rosy and optimistic to me; it feels inauthentic and insensitive. They use sayings like, "Well, at least he's in a better place," or "Now he's at peace." There is nothing wrong with a mourner using these platitudes to soothe herself, if in fact she has arrived at that place from within, but these are generally not helpful when they come from others. On the flipside, there is the dark, tragic, hopeless response to loss, which is natural and instinctive—sayings such as, "What is the point of it all in the end? Life is so cruel, so arbitrary... We're all going to end up in the ground, and then what difference does anything make?" Again, if these thoughts are generated by the person who is in pain and are part of a process he needs to go through, far be it from the rest of us to judge. Yet, as a principle, a doctrine, this tends to be depressing and unproductive in the long run.

Rabbi Leder's book is divided into three sections: *Surviving, Healing, and Growing*. He first describes how the immediate challenge after great loss is to **survive**. He says that virtually any parent he has met who has lost a child has expressed the wish to die as well. While completely understandable, to act on this urge, or to stay in this place long term, would be *below* the Horizon of Healthy Function.

Beyond the immediate need to simply survive the agony comes the challenge of **healing**. When we lose those we love, there are generally others who need us to live and be present. For them, and for ourselves, we can strive to find some degree of healing. Healing is an honest acknowledgement of the loss and correlates to being *on* the Horizon of Healthy Function.

Finally, there is the possibility for **growth**. This is the greatest challenge and demands the most energy, effort, and time. Yet these are the people who inspire the world—those who've managed to take the sourest lemons and create beauty and goodness, restoring our faith in humanity and in life. This is functioning *above* our Horizon.

Rabbi Leder's book was about loss, but this model can be applied to any area of pain or challenge. When dealing with disappointment, obstacles, curveballs, illness, injury, failure—any of the stumbling blocks that we humans inevitably encounter— we have essentially three possibilities:

1. **White flag (*below* the Horizon):** Surrender to the despair, go under, give up, become depressed or bitter.

2. **Acceptance (*on* the Horizon):** Deal with the new reality as it is by making the necessary adjustments and shifting gears.

3. **Resilience (*above* the Horizon):** Take stock of the situation, reevaluate, recalculate, and assess the possibility and potential going forward. Discern what can be learned, what can be achieved, and how can we utilize the experience.

The beauty of this model is that it is as applicable to minor setbacks as it is to major calamities. Examples of all these typologies abound in the world around us, and we tend to admire those who model the resilience.

<u>Pulling it all Together:</u>

Remember the story of King Solomon and his ring? This too shall pass. Whether we feel high or low, despondent or euphoric, there will always be more moments, more opportunities to think, feel, act and do things better each day. It took me a couple of years to muster the confidence to put this book out there. I may have the formula and words for the horizon technique, but in my own psyche and life, I'm still very much a work in progress. I'm grateful to have roadmaps, books, theories, mentors, and loved ones to help me when I'm down, and I hope you have the same.

It seems fitting that I end this book by illustrating how I'm trying to lift my own anxiety about publishing from *below* to *above* the Horizon of Healthy Thought:

1. ***Below* the Horizon:** "Even if I was able write all these words, how do I know they will be helpful or well received? There are so many books out there! Who do I think I am that my words should make a difference? And I don't even know the first thing about finding an agent, editor, or publisher… then there's my phobia of marketing and self-promotion... Where's the Hershey section, please?"

2. ***On* the Horizon:** "Writing the text is just the first hurdle. I'm still wondering whether anyone will want to read it and how to go about taking it from my Word document file to book form.

There is still a lot more to do if I want to see this project through to completion."

3. **Too High (Unhelpful Positivity)**: "I've done it! This is it— it's going to be a best-seller; I just know it. I'm just about done—now just the simple matter of getting published. It'll be flying off the shelves in no time."

4. ***Above* the Horizon:** "It feels really good to see all these pages completed. I sincerely believe and hope these ideas can make a difference. I know that writing first drafts is what comes the most easily to me in this process, so I really need to push myself to take the next steps. Researching the process of publishing and marketing is the next challenge, but I hope and pray that with the right efforts, attitude, and support, this can get completed and get out there to help others think and function more healthily and productively, the way it helps me."

Thank you so much for joining me in celebrating my 40th, and especially for staying until the end of the party. I really and humbly hope that I can join you in the celebration of your life through these words and ideas. And that whether you are 20, 40, 60, 80, or any other age, you can use some of this gift, too, to find and cultivate your own living above the Horizon of Healthy Function.

For more about the horizon of healthy thinking and writings by the author, to contact her, please visit: <u>ElishevaLiss.com</u>

Acknowledgements

"Gratitude is the root of all things good," is something a smart person would probably say. I'm actually a little nervous to list my thanks, because it's essentially impossible to enumerate all the gifts and givers in my life. More than once, I've used a turn of phrase, or shared an insight I honestly thought was original, only to learn that I had subconsciously absorbed someone else's wisdom, and assimilated it into my consciousness as if my own. I begin by asking forgiveness from those whom I will almost definitely neglect to credit. It says in Ethics of the Fathers: "Who is wise? One who learns from everyone. I've learned much from my teachers, more from my peers, and from my students the most of all." In truth, virtually every person, every experience, every moment can be a teacher, and I strive to live my life that way, but without being too annoying about it.

I thank:

Qat Wanders, my editor, Ramy Vance, my publishing consultant, Ojedokun Daniel Olusegun, my cover designer, Lewis Howes and the Inner Circle, and Chandler Bolt and everyone over at SPS- thank you all for helping me take this from a rough manuscript to publication. Mike Parker and Ypani Guerrer, the IT dream-team who designed my website and helped me navigate the world of KDP (as in: they totally did it for me.)

To my teachers (or at least the good ones,) and to all the other mentors, instructors, and professors who dedicate their lives to educating developing minds- thank you. I complained about my schooling growing up, but I now realize the incredible privilege of being educated. I especially want to acknowledge my fifth grade teacher, Ms. Raizy Vorhand, whom I haven't seen in over 30 years, but who inspired me to try and love G-d, and to want to teach others.

To my friends: Friendship has been an incredible teacher to me. As a socially awkward child, I had to consciously (attempt to) learn interpersonal propriety. To the wonderful humans who have helped along that super-fun, un-boring, imperfect journey:

My friends since childhood: Fayge Kamelhar Hirsch and her family- my second home in high school, Aviva Hollander Esses, and her family, Yehudis Hirth Dube, Estie Schwartz Zalmanowitz, and Jen Hoffman Wise.

My Israel friends: Robin Landau Aschkenasy, who survived a year as my roommate- I'm still sorry you had to go through that. Aliza Chump Feldman- who always makes me laugh, and who took us in when we were sort of homeless. Tova Renov Katz, and her whole family- to know and love Tova is to be instantly embraced by Ruki,

Kal, and the rest of their beautiful clan. Lisa/ Leah Malka Friedman-Hershman, my kindred spirit, learning buddy, and unbelievable editor, who spent much time and talent improving this manuscript.

My local friends: Mimi and Mayer Gold, for carrying Daniel and me through some of our darkest hours, and birthing my kids' best friends. Shira and Dov Messner- our dear "always" friends and travel buddies, Chaya Soberman- my "couch" friend and processing partner. Matana Jacobs- my cheerleader friend, Chaia Frischman, my writing friend, Malka Blitz, my breath-of-fresh-air friend, Dovi Tomaszewski who gave me back the beach, and my sister-in-law. Friends we made through our kids: the Larry Laubers, the Speisers, the Kelemers, Esses and other Esses, the Edells, the Feders, the Goldsteins, Shamilzadehs, and the rest of the "village". Rabbi Eytan and Rebbetzen Aviva Feiner, and Rabbi Motty and Rebbetzen Avigayil Neuberger of Congregation Knesseth Israel, dear neighbors, friends, and communal leaders.

My first private supervisor, Rivka Twerski Ganz, and all my esteemed colleagues, clients, supervisees, readers, audiences, and listeners. The good people at Nefesh and Relief who helped grow my practice with constant referrals, and provided a forum for learning, writing and speaking. I especially thank the Nefesh Listserv folks for encouraging, promoting, and critiquing my writing. Rabbi Binyamin Babad, Dr. Gayle Bessler Twerski, Dr. David Ribner, Talli Rosenbaum, and Barry

Horowitz, who have nurtured my career and professional confidence.

My greatest teachers these days are books and online lectures. Some of my favorites, many of whom I quote in this work are (including, but not limited to, and in no particular order): Dennis Prager, Matthew Kelly, Richard Carlson, Brene Brown, Neil Pasricha, Elizabeth Gilbert, Gretchen Rubin, Daniel Pink, Steven Covey, Laura Vanderkam, Jen Sincero, Esther Perel, Terrence Real, Lewis Howes, Glenon Doyle, Tony Robbins, Donald Altman, Gabby Bernstein, Shauna Niequist, and Mary Pipher.

What a blessing family can be:

My extraordinary parents, who gave me life and values, and who earn the love and respect of almost everyone they meet, and with good reason: Mrs. Toby and Dr. Naftali Reich. I could write an entire book on what I've learned from them, but germane to this project: constant support, a love of learning, and a passion for helping people. My wonderful in-laws, Rosalyn and Ian Liss: who raised my husband, adore my kids, and always choose to see the good in us all.

My fantastic brothers and sisters in law: Dani and Shonnie Reich, Akiva and Tova Reich, Shmuel Reich, and Hak and Liza Reich. My terrific brothers-in-law and sisters-in-law: Nicky and Shuli Liss, and Gary and Yael Liss. My delightful nieces and nephews, too many to list, but all very loved.

My wonderful children: Shmuel, who forged my path to parenthood, and who correctly told me "Mom, this isn't an article- it's a book." Shmuel is our scholar in residence, who amazes me with his keen observation and intellectual curiosity. He also tends to inspire my best writing. Yehuda who always brings the fun and laughter, and with whom I learned about becoming "the best versions of ourselves". Sussy, my angelic, insightful artist, whose kindness and gentleness brighten our world, and introduced me to the magic of having a daughter. Nava, whose sensitivity and sharp mind always keep me on my toes. Nava did a great job on the first proofreading of this book. And Ahuva, my exuberant dancer, whose creativity and smiles color our world. Words can't adequately express my gratitude and love for these amazing little people we are blessed to raise. You guys are the music of my life, the light within my soul. I know this work has taken some time from the family, but I've tried to make sure we still had plenty for us. I thank each of you for your support, and I hope that you guys seeing me be able to manifest these dreams, will inspire you to lead fulfilling lives according to your own inner compasses.

My dear husband, Daniel- my partner, provider, protector, IT guy, and constant companion on this wild ride. We've been through so much together- this is the year that we've been together for over half my lifetime. Thank you for helping me with the Stuff I'm Not Good At, for encouraging me to keep going when I hit a wall, for insisting that we fix the house when it was broken, and for always pushing me to invest in myself and my career, even (and especially) when I want to be cheap about it. Thank you also, for planning the most fabulous family trips- I'm so grateful to you for allowing us to make beautiful, inspiring memories all over the world, before the kids leave the nest.

Most importantly, I whole-heartedly thank my Creator; whatever I have, whatever I am, whatever I do, is there but for the grace of God, and I pray these humble efforts are blessed and bring light to others.

For more about the horizon of healthy thinking and writings by the author please visit: ElishevaLiss.com

Printed in Great Britain
by Amazon